THE LION AND THE ROCK

*"The mighty Rock is the very image
of an enormous lion, crouched between the Atlantic and the Mediterranean, and set there to guard the
passage for its British mistress"*

—THACKERAY

with map and 29 illustrations

THE LION
AND THE ROCK

The Story of the Rock of Gibraltar

DON LAWSON

ABELARD-SCHUMAN · LONDON · NEW YORK · TORONTO

This book is dedicated
to one of nature's noblemen,
Charlie Molloy,
and to his good wife,
Louise

BOOKS BY DON LAWSON

FAMOUS AMERICAN POLITICAL FAMILIES

FRANCES PERKINS, First Lady of the Cabinet

THE LION AND THE ROCK The Story of the Rock of Gibraltar

THE UNITED STATES IN THE KOREAN WAR

THE UNITED STATES IN WORLD WAR I The Story of General
John J. Pershing and the American Expeditionary Forces

THE UNITED STATES IN WORLD WAR II Crusade for
World Freedom

THE WAR OF 1812 America's Second War for Independence

YOUNG PEOPLE IN THE WHITE HOUSE

© Copyright 1969 by Don Lawson
Library of Congress Catalogue Card Number: 69-17553
Standard Book Number: 200.71618.2

LONDON	NEW YORK	TORONTO
Abelard-Schuman	Abelard-Schuman	Abelard-Schuman
Limited	Limited	Canada Limited
8 King St. WC2	6 West 57th St.	1680 Midland Ave.

Printed in the United States of America
Designed by The Etheredges

CONTENTS

ACKNOWLEDGMENTS

A number of people at Gibraltar were extremely co-operative in helping me obtain historical information and photographs for this book. Several of them I wish particularly to thank.

The Garrison Library on the Rock is a storehouse of valuable manuscripts and books about the history of Gibraltar. Mr. E. F. E. Ryan, secretary of the Garrison Library, was especially helpful in letting me use the library during my stay on the Rock. He also supplied me with copies of back issues of the Gibraltar Chronicle, the local newspaper which has among its

lists of "firsts" the enviable record of having been the
first newspaper to report Nelson's victory at Trafalgar.

Mrs. Luz-Marie Huart, librarian at the Garrison
Library, not only patiently and successfully searched
out every reference request I made of her, but she also
volunteered other valuable sources. In private conver-
sations her knowledge of the Rock's history, past and
present, supplied me with information I could not
possibly have otherwise obtained.

A special word of thanks is also due, I feel, to
Mrs. Dorothy Ellicott, the Rock's resident historian.
Mrs. Ellicott has written several excellent books about
the Rock that are noted in the bibliography at the end
of this volume. Despite the fact that she was in the
midst of writing a book about Gibraltar's role in
the Peninsular Wars while I was working on this
volume, she unhesitatingly took valuable time out to
help me track down and obtain much material that I
needed, including pictures and picture sources.

Mr. C. Montegriffo was one of the photographers
to whom Mrs. Ellicott led me, and I am grateful to
him not only for the high quality of his work but also
for the dispatch with which he handled my requests.

DON LAWSON

ILLUSTRATIONS

10

1. LIGHTING THE TORCH

On a cold, rainy, fog-shrouded November morning in 1942, a group of high-ranking American and British Army, Navy, and Air Force staff officers were gathered at Hurn airfield near Bournemouth, England. They were waiting impatiently to take off for the Rock of Gibraltar, which was to be the command headquarters for one of the most important Allied offensives of World War II – Operation Torch, the invasion of North Africa.

Their departure had already been delayed twice, and now Major Paul Tibbets was telling General

Dwight D. Eisenhower that the ceiling-zero weather conditions were reason enough for a third delay. Major Tibbets was not only the pilot of General Eisenhower's plane, the *Red Gremlin,* but he was also the commander of the group of five other B-17 Flying Fortresses that were to make the flight to Gibraltar. Normally, it would have been up to Major Tibbets as the air commander to decide whether or not they should take off, but he was letting General Eisenhower make the decision since Ike was the recently named commander in chief of Torch.

Ike did not hesitate. D-Day for the Torch landings was less than 72 hours away.

"We *have* to go," Ike said curtly.

Five of the six Flying Fortresses took off without mishap and headed toward Gibraltar. They had not flown far before everyone aboard realized that the sixth ship had not joined the formation. For some reason it had failed to take off, and the airborne planes could not break radio silence to learn why. This sixth ship was carrying General James Doolittle, the famous American flier, who had led the first air raid on Tokyo six months earlier and who was to command the 12th Air Force in the Torch operation.

But the officers and the aerial gunners aboard the five fully armed Fortresses that were now airborne had little time to be concerned about Jimmie Doolittle being left behind. They were too busy worrying about crashing into the sea that was occasionally visible just a hundred feet below. It was impossible to fly at any greater altitude because of the dense fog. This dangerous wave-hopping continued for several hours. Then, suddenly, the sun began to break through the overcast, and the ceiling gradually lifted. But the ordeal was far from over. As the Fortresses neared Gibraltar, a German Ju-88 threatened to attack the formation. The gunners aboard the B-17s were alerted, and several Spitfire fighter planes scrambled from Gibraltar's single airstrip to intercept the attacker. In a matter of minutes the Ju-88 was driven off.

As the Fortresses prepared to land, however, they were delayed by the great amount of Allied fighter-plane traffic on the lone runway. (There were some 650 Spitfires stationed on the Rock at this time.) In addition, severe crosscurrents of wind made landing difficult.

Major Tibbets circled the Rock for almost an hour, once again at wave-top height to avoid enemy aircraft, as he waited for the four other Fortresses to land. This additional delay caused rumors to circulate in London that General Eisenhower's plane had been shot down.

Finally it was Major Tibbets' turn to bring in the *Red Gremlin.* The crosscurrents of wind briefly stopped blowing, and Major Tibbets took his ship up over the Rock, then nosed down for a landing. The big bomber's wheels touched down, and the *Red Gremlin* rolled to a safe stop.

Heaving a sigh of relief, Major Tibbets said, "That's the first time I ever had to *climb* to land on

The Gibraltar airstrip, where Eisenhower landed. The Spanish coast can be seen in the background.—C. MONTEGRIFFO

a runway at the end of a flight!" (As a Colonel near the end of World War II, Paul Tibbets was to pilot the B-29 called *Enola Gay,* which dropped the first atomic bomb on Japan.)

Ike's plane was immediately surrounded by Allied officers and men, who were on hand to screen him from view by Spanish observers at the Spanish town of La Linea, just a few hundred yards from the airfield. Some weeks before, Ike had been warned in a report from the British Governor of Gibraltar, General F. Mason-MacFarlane, that everything that took place on the Rock was seen by these Spanish spies and reported to Adolf Hitler's high command in Berlin within 24 hours. Technically Spain was a neutral nation, but her sympathies were with the Axis powers.

Recalling Governor Mason-MacFarlane's words, Ike removed his cap before he stepped down from the plane. He also allowed the welcoming party to crowd around him and hide his general's stars.

General Eisenhower was hurried into a waiting staff car and then driven to Government House, where Governor Mason-MacFarlane and his staff were waiting to greet him. Government House was a former convent built for the Franciscan Friars in 1531, but Ike was not too interested in his surroundings. He was much more concerned about what had happened to General Doolittle back in England.

Ike soon learned, via coded radio messages, that the failure of Doolittle's plane to take off had been caused by faulty brakes, and that plans were under way for him to take off in another plane the next day.

Doolittle did take off safely, but the flight again almost ended in tragedy when his Fortress was attacked by three Ju-88s, several hundred miles off

the Spanish coast. The B-17's copilot was shot in the
arm, and the ship was liberally sprinkled with bullet
holes. However, the gunners managed to shoot down
one of the German attackers, and the two others were
driven off.

With Jimmie Doolittle safely on the Rock, last-
minute preparations for Operation Torch could get
under way.

The decision to invade North Africa had been
made in the spring of 1942 by President Franklin D.
Roosevelt and British Prime Minister Winston Churchill at a meeting in Washington. Earlier, it had been
hoped that the Allies would soon be able to open a
second front somewhere on the European continent
which, at this time, was held in the iron grip of Nazi
Germany and Fascist Italy.

When it became clear that a mass invasion of
Europe across the English Channel was not yet
possible — the United States had only been at war with
the Axis powers since December 7, 1941 — a second
front in Africa was suggested. There, German General
Erwin Rommel's *Afrika Korps* was threatening to over-
run the British forces at El Alamein and capture the
Suez Canal. In addition, it was felt that almost any
full-scale Allied offensive in the Atlantic theater of war
would relieve some of the German pressure that was
threatening to destroy Marshal Joseph Stalin's armies
on the Russian front.

As soon as the joint Anglo-American invasion of
North Africa was decided upon and General Eisen-

hower was named the Torch commander in chief, intense preparations began in both the United States and Great Britain. Overall strategy for the operation was planned in London by the Joint Chiefs of Staff and troops were trained for the invasion on both sides of the Atlantic.

On October 24, 1942 — more than a week before General Eisenhower and his staff flew to their headquarters at Gibraltar — a convoy of infantry and armored troops sailed from the United States. In command of these troops was the colorful General George S. (Blood and Guts) Patton. On October 25 a combined force of Anglo-American combat troops sailed from England — the largest amphibious operation in the history of warfare up to this time. It was also the most complicated.

The two vast fleets carrying about 100,000 soldiers — three-quarters of them American — had to rendezvous in the Straits of Gibraltar off the coast of Africa at precisely the right hour. They then had to coordinate their movements so that troops could be disembarked simultaneously at Casablanca in Morocco and Algiers and Oran in Algeria. In addition, air support had to arrive on a split-second schedule from Gibraltar.

All of these problems, plus a hundred others, had to be dealt with by General Eisenhower and his staff during the short time that remained before the invasion. Although Ike's living quarters were at Government House in the former convent on Gibraltar's main street, his working headquarters and war room were a half mile inside a tunnel that had been blasted out of the Rock itself.

After the war Ike said that Gibraltar had made the Allied invasion of Africa possible. He added, however, that his headquarters and war room just off the so-called Admiralty tunnel were the most dismal of any he had during the entire war. Despite the best efforts of technicians to supply adequate electricity, the tunnel was dark and gloomy, the air was dank and foul and there was a constant dripping of water from the rock ceiling. Nevertheless, signal equipment for communicating with the Joint Chiefs of Staff, as well as with the assault forces and their vital air cover, was set up and seemed to be in excellent working order.

General Eisenhower was considerably cheered when he received a special message of faith and encouragement from Prime Minister Winston Churchill. To launch Operation Torch, Churchill had given Ike temporary command of the Rock of Gibraltar, making the American General the first "foreign" commander of Britain's proud fortress in almost two-and-a-half centuries. The message from Churchill read:

THE ROCK IS SAFE IN YOUR HANDS!

Perhaps prompted by Churchill's message, General Eisenhower and one of his aides left the Admiralty tunnel on the afternoon before D-Day and took off

A *Barbary ape*—FIELD MUSEUM OF NATURAL HISTORY

on a strange mission. They drove halfway up the steep slopes of Gibraltar in search of a band of apes that lived there.

No one knew where these Barbary, or Rock, apes originally came from, but according to tradition as long as they remained on Gibraltar the British would keep control of the Rock. Several times in the past the apes had been threatened with extinction. Once, during World War II, their number decreased alarmingly. When Winston Churchill learned of this he took time out from his war duties to order that the number of apes on the Rock be increased. This was done by

capturing the animals in Spanish Morocco, one of the
former Barbary states from which the apes got their
name, and transporting them to Gibraltar.

General Eisenhower finally found several of the
Rock apes nibbling away at the foliage. Ike managed
to get close enough to pat one on the head for good
luck. The General and his aide then drove back to
headquarters to wait and worry through the long,
dark hours before D-Day and H-Hour of Operation
Torch.

One of Ike's greatest worries was caused by the
extremely complicated political situation involved in
the invasion. Most of North Africa was occupied by
the only Free French military forces that were left
after Hitler had taken over France early in the war.
It was hoped that the French military leaders and
government officials in North Africa would greet the
invaders as liberators, but this was by no means
certain. Many French officers in Africa continued to
be loyal to Marshal Henri Pétain and his puppet
French government back at Vichy in France. This
government at Vichy had been set up in 1940, after
the fall of France, by splitting France into a northern
half occupied by the Germans, and a southern half
occupied by the French. Marshal Pétain, who collabo-
rated fully with Nazi Germany and adopted many of
Hitler's police-state methods, was in charge of the
Vichy government in southern France.

Shortly after dawn on the morning of November 8,
1942 — less than a year after the Japanese attack on
Pearl Harbor had brought the United States into the

war — more than 800 warships, troop transports and cargo carriers began disembarking combat troops at the three invasion points in Morocco and Algeria. Simultaneously, 14 squadrons of fighter planes arrived from Gibraltar, which had become the hub of the great wheel around which the whole invasion turned. From his command post on Gibraltar, General Eisenhower immediately began to receive reports on the progress of the invasion at Algiers and Oran. Because of last-minute radio failure, no news was received from Casablanca.

The American forces landing at Algiers, Ike and his staff learned, had met with only token resistance from the French. At Oran resistance was somewhat stiffer. A division of paratroops was ordered to make its first combat jump at Oran, and there the situation was soon brought under Allied control.

When still no word was heard from Casablanca, aircraft were dispatched to try and make contact. These planes were shot down. Finally, a fast ship was sent, and it was soon learned that the assault forces at Casablanca were safely ashore despite the fact that they had had to land under intense artillery fire from coastal batteries and a French warship. Tank columns had moved out to surround Casablanca and prepare for a siege, if necessary. General Patton assured Ike that would not be necessary. He was right — by November 11 all resistance had ceased.

As message after message flashed into General Eisenhower's command post on the Rock, it became increasingly clear that the enemy had been taken

An Allied convoy off the Rock during World War II—CANADIAN
GEOGRAPHICAL JOURNAL

completely by surprise — the great gamble of Operation Torch had paid off handsomely.

Ike and his staff immediately began to make plans for reinforcing the invasion troops. These plans moved forward so swiftly that within a few weeks 200,000 men, more than 20,000 vehicles and several hundred tons of supplies were safely landed at the three invasion points. Also 1,500 miles of territory were in Allied hands. What was more, Rommel, the "Desert Fox," was about to be caught in a trap between the Torch invaders on the west and British General Bernard Montgomery's Eighth Army on the east. In addition, the Allies would soon have a firm base for attacking Southern Europe.

General Eisenhower returned the command of Gibraltar to Governor Mason-MacFarlane on November 23 and transferred his headquarters to Algiers. Although this may not have occurred to Ike, he had actually been the 71st commander of the Rock since its capture by the British in 1704. His "term of office" was undoubtedly shorter than any of the 70 governors, lieutenant governors or commandants who preceded him, but during the few days that the Rock was under Ike's command the whole course of World War II was changed. Churchill called the Torch victory "not the end, not the beginning of the end, but the end of the beginning" of the war.

It was not the first time the Rock of Gibraltar had played a key role in altering history. It had been playing that role since its beginnings back in ancient times.

2. THE PILLARS OF HERCULES

The early Greeks and Romans believed that the mighty Hercules, son of the god Zeus, built the great rocky headlands that still stand on either side of the Straits of Gibraltar and guard the mouth of the Mediterranean Sea. These huge headlands were called the Pillars of Hercules, and the Greeks and Romans feared to sail beyond them from the Mediterranean into the Atlantic Ocean. Today, the Pillar of Hercules on the narrow peninsula near the southern tip of Spain is Gibraltar, and the Pillar opposite Gibraltar across the Straits holds the Spanish town of Ceuta.

The Pillars of Hercules were originally called
Mons Calpe on the Gibraltar side and Mons Abyla
across the Straits. Early pictures showed the two pillars
bound together by a scroll bearing the Latin words
Ne plus ultra, meaning, "no more beyond." Later,
Spanish pieces-of-eight bore the pillars-and-scroll de-
sign, and it is probably from this that we get the
American dollar ($) symbol.

Gibraltar was first used as a fortress after the year
711 A.D.* In that year 12,000 Arab troops led by
Tarik-ben-Zeyad, a Persian army commander in the
service of the Moors who had conquered North Africa,
sailed from Ceuta across the Straits to invade Spain.
Tarik and his men landed without opposition at Mons
Calpe and occupied the Rock. Shortly afterwards Mons
Calpe was renamed Gibel-Tarik, meaning the hill or
mountain of Tarik. The name Gibel-Tarik gradually
became the present Gibraltar.

The warrior Tarik was quick to see Gibraltar's
advantages as a natural fortress. The peninsula on
which the Rock is situated is about three miles long
from north to south and somewhat less than a mile
wide. It covers about two and one-quarter square miles,
making it in modern times the second smallest of Great
Britain's possessions. (The smallest is Pitcairn Island,
covering about one and three-quarters square miles.)

---

* *H. W. Howes, former Director of Education at Gibraltar,
divides the history of the Rock into four major periods: (1) Pre-
711 A.D.; (2) Moorish Domination, 711-1461; (3) Spanish
Occupation, 1462-1703; (4) British Rule, 1704 to the present.*

Locking the gates of Gibraltar—ILLUSTRATED LONDON NEWS

*A night view of the floodlit
north face of the Rock*—C. MONTEGRIFFO

The narrow isthmus leading from Spain to the northern tip of the Rock of Gibraltar itself is a flat stretch of sandy ground just a few feet above sea level, and is the location of the North Point airfield, where Ike landed. South of the isthmus the great limestone Rock rises almost straight up to a height of more than a thousand feet. From the north end of the Rock a ridge rises even higher — to about 1,400 feet* — commanding a majestic view of the Straits, the Bay of Gibraltar and the Mediterranean Sea. This ridge, or backbone, then slopes gradually southward toward the sea.

On the east side of the Rock a sheer cliff drops down 300 feet from the central ridge. The western side is less sheer, and it is here on the lower western slopes that the town and harbor were built. Most attempts to seize the Rock have been made by invading forces crossing the narrow isthmus at the north end of the peninsula or by landing from the seaward side at Europa Flats, at the extreme southern end of the peninsula. Most bombardments of the Rock have been made against its western or sea face.

Not much is known about the history of Gibraltar for several centuries after the Moors invaded the European mainland in 711, by way of Gibraltar, to conquer Spain. Between 1309 and 1462 the Moors and Spanish fought a series of eight major battles for the Rock's possession, first one side occupying the great

* About the height of New York City's Empire State building.

Spanish pieces of eight. Note Pillars of Hercules symbols from which American dollar sign was probably derived—THE AMERICAN NUMISMATIC SOCIETY

stronghold and then the other. All of this fighting was conducted in an extremely cruel form of siege warfare.

In 1435, during the seventh battle, a Spanish commander by the name of Henry de Guzman was drowned in the waters surrounding the Rock and his body was recovered by the Moors. The Spanish offered a ransom for the body of their fallen leader, but the Moors refused it. Instead they placed the body in a cage and hung it over one of the walls of a castle they had built on the Rock. There it remained in plain view of attacking armies for many years. It was during Henry de Guzman's fruitless effort to recapture the Rock that artillery was used for the first time at Gibraltar.

In 1462 Henry de Guzman's son, John, and another Spanish commander, Alonzo de Arcos, led an attack against Gibraltar that drove the Moors from the Rock for the last time. De Arcos was the newly appointed Governor of Tarifa, a Spanish port on the Strait of Gibraltar that had long been held by the Moors. Moorish or Barbary pirates based at Tarifa took a toll of ships that sailed through the Straits. If a ship's captain did not want his vessel destroyed or its contents stolen, he paid these pirates from Tarifa a fee to be allowed to proceed without harm. From this custom derived our English word "tariff."

When the Moors were finally driven from the Rock after having dominated it for 750 years, they left little behind them of a permanent nature except the Moorish Castle (the remains of which can still be seen today) and some simple fortifications. The Spanish then dominated the Rock for almost two-and-a-half centuries, during which time they attempted to turn it into a military stronghold.

The Spanish occupation of Gibraltar was not altogether serene. For many years it was a pawn in what amounted to Spanish civil warfare. For a time it was so little regarded by the Royal government of Spain that it was used as a penal colony. Finally, King

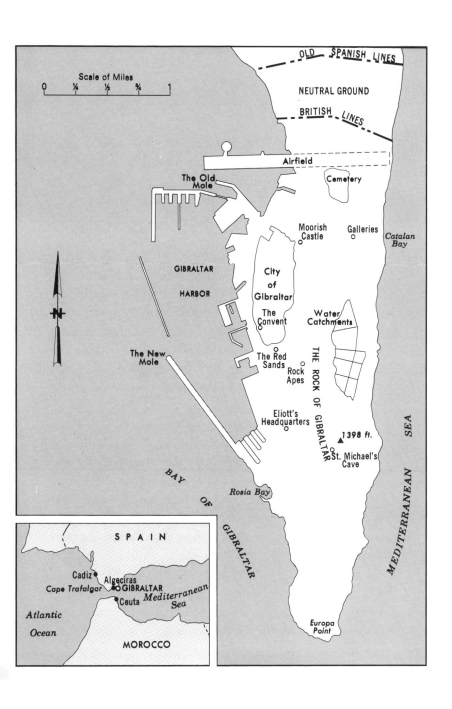

Ferdinand and Queen Isabella became aware of Gibraltar's importance as a symbol of their country's power.

Early in the 16th century, Queen Isabella gave Gibraltar a coat of arms — a castle with a golden key, indicating that the Rock was the key to Spain. When she died in 1504, Isabella left behind her a will in which she told the rulers who succeeded her to hold Gibraltar at all costs.

But Christopher Columbus had recently discovered America, and most of Isabella's successors had their eyes focused only on Spanish conquests in the New World. While they were thus occupied, the small garrison at Gibraltar had to defend the Rock against its 11th siege. This was an attack by several thousand pirates from Algiers, who fought their way ashore and sacked the town. The besiegers were eventually driven off and the Spanish kept control of the Rock.

After this near-disaster, Emperor Charles V decided to improve the Rock's system of defenses. A famous military engineer by the name of Daniel Spreckel was imported from Strassburg, and he completely replanned and rebuilt the fortifications. He did his work so well that all the European nations soon began to regard Gibraltar as a truly impregnable fortress. And so it was to remain until the start of the 18th century. Then, in 1704, during the War of the Spanish Succession, the English Admiral Sir George Rooke captured the Rock and placed it under the powerful paw of the British lion.

3. ROOKE TAKES THE ROCK

It took less than half a day for General Eisenhower, the commander in chief of the Torch operation in World War II, to fly the more than 1,100 miles from England to his headquarters at Gibraltar. After he landed he was in close radio communication with his superiors, the Joint Chiefs of Staff, back in London.

During the War of the Spanish Succession, when Admiral Sir George Rooke was commander in chief of the expedition that captured the Rock for the British, it took a fleet of men-of-war more than 30 days to sail from Great Britain to Gibraltar. Rooke, of course, had no radio or any other means of quick communication with his superiors, the Lords of the Admiralty, in London. Once Rooke was out of sight of land, he was virtually on his own when it came to making battle decisions. This fact was to be of great importance in the British capture of Gibraltar.

The War of the Spanish Succession began in 1701. It grew out of a dispute over who should rule Spain, and that country's vast possessions, following the death of the childless Spanish King, Charles II, in 1700. King Charles had left the throne to his great-nephew, Philip, a member of the French royal family.

Philip's claim to the Spanish throne was hotly disputed by several European nations that supported the Archduke Charles of Austria's claim to the throne. Britain, fearing that a union between France and Spain would destroy the balance of power in Europe, was one of the nations supporting Charles's claim. England declared war against France and Spain in 1702.

Once the war began, it engulfed not only the whole of Western Europe but also spread to America, where it was known as Queen Anne's War because Queen Anne was then on the English throne. In America, the contest was between France and England over who should rule the North American continent. Allied against the Spanish and French in Europe were England, Prussia and Austria (today's Germany), the Netherlands and Portugal.

Shortly after England declared war in the spring of 1702, Sir George Rooke was named commander in chief of an expedition against the Spanish coastal city of Cadiz. Rooke was a career naval officer who had seen much active service in earlier wars in which he had won distinction. He had been knighted in 1690 for having destroyed a fleet of French men-of-war, and had more recently been named Vice Admiral of England. No English naval officer had a higher reputation than Sir George Rooke at this time. Nevertheless, the expedition he led against Cadiz was a complete failure despite the fact that he had some 50 English and Dutch men-of-war at his command, as well as a number of smaller vessels and about 14,000 soldiers or marines.

He partly made up for the failure to capture Cadiz when, on the return voyage to England, he intercepted a squadron of Spanish and French warships convoying several treasure ships from the West Indies to Spain. Rooke destroyed the convoy in the harbor at Vigo on the Spanish coast, and captured gold and silver valued at millions of pounds, which he brought back to England.

In the autumn of 1703, Rooke was sent to Holland to escort Austrian Archduke Charles to Lisbon where, as the new king, he could begin to assert his authority over the Iberian peninsula. This expedition had to be delayed when a severe storm struck the Dutch coast, while the grand fleet was still in harbor, and many vessels were either destroyed or badly damaged.

Early in 1704, Rooke left with part of the fleet to take the Austrian pretender to the Spanish Crown to

Spain. Accompanying the expedition was the German Prince George of Hesse-Darmstadt, who was in charge of the English and Dutch marines. The Prince was convinced that many of the Spanish people were ready to recognize the Austrian Archduke Charles as their king and would do so if the grand fleet landed a strong force of marines at Barcelona.

This proved to be a completely mistaken notion. The garrison at Barcelona fought off all attacks by the marine landing forces, and Admiral Rooke had to take part personally in the hand-to-hand fight to help the Allied troops get back on board their ships.

Shortly after the failure of the Barcelona amphibious assault, Rooke sailed to Lisbon, where late in June he was reinforced by additional men-of-war under the command of Britain's Sir Cloudesley Shovell. This combined fleet was a truly powerful one, consisting of 59 English and Dutch ships of the line as well as a number of smaller vessels. But it was in a sense a powerless fleet because its commander had no orders from the Admiralty regarding the exact nature of his next mission.

Lacking specific orders, Rooke could not make up his mind whether to attack Barcelona or Cadiz again, or simply to sail about the Mediterranean waiting for word from the Admiralty and looking for the French war squadron. In the end he continued cruising about aimlessly for some weeks.

Admiral Rooke was aware, of course, that with such a large and powerful fighting force at his

command he could hardly return to England without
having gained a victory of some kind. He was also
aware that his failures in the war up to now had
added no luster to his reputation.

Finally, late in July, Admiral Rooke held a council
of war with his top officers aboard the flagship *Royal
Catherine*. Several schemes were discussed for doing
"something of importance." Rooke pointed out that
since the start of the war the Allies had known that,
in order to keep control of the western Mediterranean,
attempts would have to be made to take Cadiz,
Barcelona or Gibraltar. The attempts on Cadiz and
Barcelona having failed, only one other key stronghold
remained as a possibility. After some debate it was
decided by Rooke and his flag officers to attempt to
take Gibraltar.

The immediate reasons given for the attack were
(1) it was believed that the Spanish had recently been
keeping only a small garrison in the fortress; (2) possession of Gibraltar would help win the War of the
Spanish Succession, and (3) taking the Rock might
persuade the Spaniards to accept Archduke Charles of
Austria as their king.

This was not the first time that specific plans had
been made by an English admiral to capture Gibraltar.
Half a century earlier, in 1656, an admiral named
Montague had written to Oliver Cromwell saying that
Gibraltar was a place that could be of great use to
the British "in case it could be reduced." The only way
of reducing — that is, taking — it, he added, was "to

land a body of forces on the isthmus and thereby cut off communications of the town with the mainland and in this situation make a brisk attack upon the place" — "the place" meaning the fortress and town. Although this suggestion had come to nothing in Cromwell's time, it is quite possible that a naval career officer like Admiral Rooke would have read or heard of the plan and remembered it. In any event, it was a plan that he substantially adopted at this point.

On July 21, 1704, the 11th siege of Gibraltar began. Admiral Rooke moved his war fleet into the Bay of Gibraltar and immediately began to disembark the Prince of Hesse-Darmstadt's force of 1,800 English and Dutch marines "on the neck of land to the northward of the town." The town and its surrounding fortress were thus cut off from contact with the mainland.

Rooke then moved his fleet farther south to attack the western face of the Rock. Gibraltar's fortifications at this time consisted mainly of a great stone wall that was meant to protect the town from just such an attack from the west. Mounted all along the top of this castle-like wall was artillery, and at either end were heavily armed strongpoints.

As the siege began, Admiral Rooke called upon the Spanish Governor of Gibraltar, General Diego de Salinas, to surrender in the name of "Charles III, King of Spain." The Governor flatly refused. Rooke then ordered his ships' captains to prepare to bombard the fortress, but an unfavorable wind made it difficult for the ships to maneuver into favorable positions in the shallow inshore waters of the Bay. The Bay was in fact so shallow that the flagship had only a foot-and-a-half of water under its keel.

During this one-day delay Admiral Rooke, "to amuse the enemy," as he put it with a warrior's hard humor, "sent in Captain Edward Whitaker with some boats who burnt a French privateer of 12 guns anchored at the New Mole." The New Mole was a man-made breakwater at the south end of the fortress wall. Another breakwater called the Old Mole was at the wall's north end.

The actual bombardment of the fortress began at dawn on Sunday, July 23, 1704. Rooke had lined up his fleet just a few hundred yards from the western face of the Rock, and for the next four or five hours his ships' gunners poured more than 15,000 cannonballs into the beleaguered fortress. The attackers aboard their ships could soon see that "the enemy were beat from their guns."

Rooke then sent in 3,000 British marines and sailors in landing craft under the command of Captain Whitaker, but when they landed on the New Mole the Spanish defenders blew up a powder magazine there, killing more than 100 Allied officers and men. The storming party continued to advance, however, and soon the outer fortifications and the town itself were in their hands. Meanwhile, the Prince of Hesse-Darmstadt and his marines were successfully breaching the fortress walls from the north, or isthmus, end of the Rock.

Before nightfall Gibraltar was under Allied control. The Governor agreed to surrender by eight o'clock the next morning. That night the city was plundered by the victorious English and Dutch troops.

The next day, July 24, 1704, Gibraltar was formally surrendered in the name of Charles III, to whom the defeated soldiers and civilians had to take an oath of allegiance. Admiral Rooke announced that no harm would come to any of the 6,000 civilians who wanted to remain, but most of them left the Rock taking whatever possessions they could carry with them. The 150 Spanish soldiers were allowed to leave, taking with them several cannon, a dozen cannonballs for each gun and enough food to last each man a week.

After Rooke's success in taking Gibraltar, the French asserted that the Spanish had had neither a garrison nor guns on the Rock. This obviously was not true. Rooke in his report to the Admiralty said, "The town is extremely strong and had 100 guns mounted which were well supplied with ammunition." Allied military officers who later inspected the fortifications stated flatly, "50 men might have defended those works against thousands. Gibraltar only fell because there never was such an attack as those seamen made."

The truth was that the Rock had not been stoutly defended by its small garrison. Even so, Rooke's forces suffered more than 300 casualties in the attack, and the casualties would have been much higher if the Spaniards had put up anything but token resistance.

Although the official surrender was made in the

name of Charles III, Admiral Rooke ordered the royal standard of Great Britain to be raised over the Rock, and Gibraltar was occupied in the name of Queen Anne. As it happened, however, the first Governor of Gibraltar after Admiral Rooke captured it for the British was a German and the second Governor was a Spaniard. A British Governor was not to take over for two more years, and Britain was not to have any legal claim to the Mediterranean stronghold until the Treaty of Utrecht was signed in 1713, at the end of the War of the Spanish Succession.

4. "SAFE AS THE ROCK
OF GIBRALTAR"

A week after the capture of Gibraltar, Admiral Rooke and his naval forces left the Rock and went in search of the French war fleet. The Prince of Hesse-Darmstadt remained behind as Governor of Gibraltar — the first Governor under British rule of the Rock — as well as commander of the garrison of 3,000 marines.

Early in August, Rooke encountered the French fleet off Malaga. The fight that followed was a fierce one, lasting from midmorning on August 13 to early evening. Both sides suffered severe losses in men and ships, and afterwards both sides claimed victory. Actually, neither won.

Then, for the first time, Gibraltar proved its great value as a refuge for British warships. After the bloody but indecisive battle with the French fleet, Rooke brought his battered ships back to Gibraltar. There they remained for a week undergoing repairs and taking on provisions for the long voyage back to England. Before he left for home, Rooke had 60 cannons removed from his ships and hauled ashore to strengthen the Rock's defenses.

When he arrived in England late in September, Admiral Rooke received very little public acclaim for his capture of Gibraltar. This was partly due to political reasons — Rooke supported the party that was out of power — but mainly it was because the public was not yet fully aware of Gibraltar's importance as the key to the Mediterranean. Many persons, both in and out of Parliament, regarded the Rock as a useless acquisition.

Queen Anne, however, invited the Admiral to Windsor Castle, where she congratulated him and promised to present him with a golden cup and perhaps even give him a dukedom. He was never given either. In fact, soon after Rooke returned to England, his conduct of certain naval battles — particularly against the French off Malaga — was seriously questioned, and he was removed as commander in chief.

He was never again recalled to active service. Admiral Sir George Rooke retired on half pay at Canterbury, where in 1708 he died, a lonely and all-but-forgotten man.

If the English showed mild reaction to the capture

of the Rock, not so the Spaniards. Almost immediately after its loss they began to mount a counterattack against the fortress. Nine thousand Spanish troops that had been fighting on the borders of Portugal were withdrawn from that front. These soldiers plus 3,000 French troops encamped on the isthmus north of the Rock early in October, 1704. In support of this combined land force of 12,000 men was a powerful French war fleet of 12 men-of-war and seven frigates. Anchored at Algeciras, across the bay from Gibraltar, they prepared to bombard the Rock. The French-Spanish counterattack began on October 9.

The small Gibraltar garrison was not unprepared for the siege — the Rock's 12th. Realizing they were without naval protection after Admiral Rooke returned to England, the Prince of Hesse-Darmstadt and his men set about strengthening the Rock's fortifications. The additional ships' guns that Rooke had left them were mounted, all the walls were repaired and several new strongpoints were built along the western sea front. Nevertheless, the onslaught that followed was a deadly one. Bombarded from the French warships in the bay as well as from the land-based cannons on the isthmus, the garrison lost a third of its defenders in three weeks.

The most serious threat to the fortress took place late in October, when 500 Spanish soldiers scaled the sheer cliff on the eastern side of the Rock. Until then this route had been considered impassable. The assault party was led by a former Gibraltar goatherd who was familiar with a generally unknown pathway up the steep east slope. This threat to their unguarded rear could have been disastrous to the Gibraltar defenders, but a boy bringing lunch to his father who was on guard duty near the top of the Rock spotted the invaders and sounded the alarm. A fierce hand-to-hand fight followed in which almost every member of the assault party was either killed or driven back over the rocky precipice.

On October 29, a squadron of 18 British warships suddenly appeared in the Bay of Gibraltar. These men-of-war were under the command of Sir John Leake and had been stationed at Lisbon with instructions to reinforce the Rock if that proved necessary. Leake's fleet defeated the French ships of the line in the Bay and then began to bombard the French-Spanish army on the isthmus.

The strength of the Gibraltar garrison had gone down to about 1,500 men, disease as well as shot and shell having taken its toll of the defenders. Admiral Leake landed reinforcements of 500 sailors as well as additional supplies before he had to return to Lisbon for ammunition and stores.

The bitter siege continued until the early spring of 1705. Several times during the winter months Admiral Leake returned to reinforce the Rock, and finally he landed a major force of several thousand British regulars. By this time the besiegers were also suffering severely from disease. With Admiral Leake's fleet in full command of the Bay and the Gibraltar

garrison stronger than it had ever been, the disheart-
ened Spanish and French marched away from the
isthmus in April, leaving the British royal standard still
flying over the fortress. British forces had successfully
completed their first defense of Gibraltar — but it was
not to be the last.

During the six months of the siege 80,000 gunshots
and cannon shells had been fired into the fortress. The
brave garrison lost perhaps half of its original strength
of 3,000 men, but the besiegers suffered 10,000 casualties from wounds and disease.

Before the siege was many weeks old, the public
back in England had become fully aware of the ordeal
the Rock's defenders were undergoing. When the siege
was finally lifted, there was great rejoicing in London,
and it was from this time on that the legend of
Gibraltar's invincibility began to grow. "Safe as the
Rock of Gibraltar" was a phrase that was soon heard
around the world.

During the summer after the siege was lifted, the
Austrian Archduke Charles, who was still pressing his
claim to the throne of Spain, visited Gibraltar. He and
the Prince of Hesse-Darmstadt soon left on an expedition against Barcelona, leaving behind as Governor not
a British commander but a Spanish general by the
name of Ramos who had been serving with the Allies —
the second Governor under British rule. The Prince of
Hesse-Darmstadt was later killed in the attack against
Barcelona.

The War of the Spanish Succession drew to a close

in 1713, after the French were defeated in a series of European land battles. Because the Archduke Charles had become Emperor of Austria in 1711, it seemed logical to the other European powers that not Charles but the French claimant to the throne, Philip, should be recognized as the new King of Spain. This the Allies agreed to on condition that Spain and France never again be united in peace or war. A treaty to this effect was signed at Utrecht in the Netherlands in 1713.

A key part of the Treaty of Utrecht was Article 10. It was under this article that Britain gained legal and lasting right to Gibraltar. It read as follows:

"Article 10.   The Catholic King does hereby for himself, his heirs and successors, yield to the Crown of Great Britain the full and entire property of the town and castle of Gibraltar, together with the port, fortifications, and forts thereunto belonging; and he gives up the said property to be held and enjoyed absolutely with all manner of right forever, without any exceptions or impediment whatsoever."

Despite the blunt clarity of this statement, it was not long before the Spanish were demanding the return of Gibraltar. When these demands failed, the Spanish again launched a full-scale assault against the fortress. This effort in 1727 — the Rock's 13th siege — also failed. Spain's diplomatic as well as military efforts to regain the Rock continued to meet with failure for the next half-century.

Then, at the start of the last quarter of the 18th century, Britain was faced with the problem of putting down a revolt in her American colonies. With Britain fully engaged in the War of American Independence, Spain launched her most powerful attack against Gibraltar. This resulted in the 14th and most famous siege in the Rock's long and embattled history — the Great Siege of 1779-83.

5. THE GREAT SIEGE BEGINS

The year 1776 was as important a milestone in the history of the Rock of Gibraltar as it was in the history of the United States.

When the 13 American colonies declared their independence from Britain on July 4, 1776, Spain began planning to take advantage of Britain's preoccupation with the rebellion in America to try to repossess Gibraltar. What the English needed was an experienced military man to take command of the Mediterranean fortress and prepare its defenses against Spanish attack. They got just such a man in

Lieutenant-General George Augustus Eliott, a lifelong
professional soldier.

General Eliott was 59 years old and a veteran of
many military campaigns when he took over as
Gibraltar's 28th Governor. Both his combat and ad-
ministrative experience had ideally equipped him for
commanding the Gibraltar garrison under siege.

Eliott was not a handsome man. He was tall,
heavy-set and had a large beaklike nose and black,
bushy eyebrows. He cared little, however, about his
looks or what people thought of him personally. He
did care greatly about the results he obtained in battle.
His stern eyes and equally stern mouth clearly indicated that he was a strict commanding officer — but
he was also a fair one. He was, in fact, no more strict
with his troops than he was with himself. He led a
Spartan life both on and off the battlefield, seldom
sleeping more than four hours a night. Unlike most
soldiers of his time, he drank nothing but water and
ate no meat. Although Eliott was not a man who was
greatly loved by those who served with or under him,
his self-discipline and his dedication to his soldier's
job were greatly respected and admired.

George Augustus Eliott was born — ironically for
one who was to become one of his nation's famed
military men — on Christmas Day in the village of
Stobs, Scotland, in 1717. He was the seventh son of Sir
Gilbert Eliott, a titled but poor Scottish aristocrat.
From the time he was a small boy, young Eliott
wanted to become a soldier. He received his early

*A huge statue of General Eliott stands in the patio of the con-
vent. The keys of the fortress, which he holds, were carved
from the bowsprit of an enemy warship captured at Trafalgar.*
COURTESY MRS. DOROTHY ELLICOTT

schooling at Leyden in the Netherlands and then attended the French military academy at La Fère. As a boy in his teens he volunteered to fight with the Prussian army in 1735 and 1736, during the almost constant European warfare that was then going on.

When he returned to England in 1737, Eliott enrolled for military classes at Woolwich and was later commissioned in the English army as an officer in the field engineers. During the War of the Austrian Succession, Lieutenant Eliott served with the British Grenadier Guards and was wounded at the Battle of Dettingen. He emerged from the war a captain.

In 1748 he married into a rich and famous family. His wife, Anne, was the daughter of a descendant of England's great sea captain of the Elizabethan Age, Sir Francis Drake. The Eliotts had two children, a daughter, Anne, and a son, Francis, who also followed an army career.

In 1754 Eliott obtained a commission as a lieutenant colonel. King George II, the last British ruler to lead his troops in battle, made Eliott his aide at the start of the Seven Years' War in 1756. (In America this conflict was called the French and Indian War.) Eliott's ability to speak French and German fluently was a great help to him in his role as aide to the King.

Later in the Seven Years' War, Eliott was placed in command of the first light cavalry unit to be formed in the British army. At the head of this unit, Eliott, as a full colonel, distinguished himself in several battles. He also was noted for the great care he took to obtain the best battle equipment and most comfortable quarters for his soldiers — in days when commanding officers generally had little regard for the well-being of their troops.

In 1759, Eliott was promoted to major general. In 1762, he was sent as second in command of an expedition to Cuba, which resulted in the capture of the Cuban capital of Havana. British troops held Havana until the close of the Seven Years' War in 1763. This success brought Eliott 25,000 pounds in prize money, with which he bought an estate in Sussex.

Shortly after his wife's death in 1774, Eliott was named commander in chief of the British forces in Ireland, a relatively inactive post and the first army command Eliott had held which he did not like. He asked to be relieved of the Irish post and placed in a more active command. His request was granted and in 1776 he was promoted to lieutenant general and was named Governor of Gibraltar.

When Eliott took over active command of the Gibraltar garrison early in 1777, he found the Rock's defenses almost nonexistent. The fortifications had been neglected since the siege of 1727 and were in a state of decay and ruin. There were very few cannon mounted on the walls, and for those that were mounted there was little ammunition. Food stocks were also low and the garrison itself was below strength. Eliott estimated that 8,000 soldiers were needed to man the fortress, but he found only 3,000 on hand.

Fortunately, Eliott was to have two years in which

to set matters right, but, at that time, he had no way of knowing this. He immediately began to prepare the fortress for the anticipated siege. First he sent urgent messages to England requesting additional troops, then he began to strengthen the Rock's physical defenses.

One of the most able officers he found in the garrison was a Lieutenant Colonel of Engineers, William Green. Colonel Green, like Eliott, had attended the Royal Military Academy at Woolwich. Under Green's direction several new stone walls and strongpoints called bastions were built, and all the existing fortifications were repaired. Shore batteries of howitzers, mortars and other large guns were mounted and supplied with powder, shot and shell. Colonel Green drove his men hard, working them from dawn to dark seven days a week.

As the Rock's defenses were slowly improved, so were its food supplies and its troop strength. When his urgent messages for reinforcements were ignored, Eliott sent the Deputy Governor of Gibraltar, Lieutenant General Robert Boyd, to England to demand more men and food. New regiments were finally sent to the Rock, and the stores of meat, vegetables, fruit and flour were increased to the point where the garrison of 5,300 soldiers could be self-sufficient for many months. The civilian population of the town numbered about 4,000. Eliott had given orders for these civilians to lay in supplies to last them for six months. Not all of the townspeople did so, however.

General Eliott worked tirelessly and no detail was

too small for his attention. He not only rationed all fresh meat as the siege approached, but he also ordered his troops not to powder their hair, which was a common custom. Flour was usually used for this purpose, and General Eliott knew that every ounce of flour was going to be needed for food.

By 1779, the Revolutionary War in America had been going on for more than four years. The French had been giving the Americans much assistance in their struggle against the British. In the summer of 1779, the Spanish also decided to give indirect help to the American colonists by declaring war on Great Britain. The Spanish reached this decision not because of their love for American ideals — they actually gave the American colonists little direct aid — but because of their hatred of the British.

Spain's main aim in forming an alliance with the French against the British was to recapture Gibraltar, and France agreed to aid Spain in this effort. Soon a combined French-Spanish army of 15,000 men, under General Alvarez de Sotomayor, was encamped on the isthmus and mainland north of Gibraltar. This number later grew to 40,000 under the French Duke of Crillon, while the Gibraltar garrison never numbered more than 6,000 soldiers fit for duty. The British Gibraltar war fleet of four or five vessels was also badly outnumbered by the 80 enemy men-of-war blockading the Rock. As General Eliott had foreseen when he first arrived at Gibraltar, dark and bitter days lay ahead for him and his small, gallant garrison.

The Great Siege officially began on July 11, 1779,

but little action took place for several weeks. Early in
September General Eliott decided to shell the enemy's
advance position. Before the bombardment began he
ordered that the streets of Gibraltar be ploughed so that
when the enemy guns returned the fire from the fortress
the shells would not ricochet but would sink into
the earth. He also ordered that all of the towers in the
town be torn down to eliminate targets for the enemy
gunners.

At dawn on Sunday, September 13, a major
bombardment of the siege was begun by the British.
The first shot against the Spanish lines was fired when
a Mrs. Skinner, the wife of an officer, took a flaming
torch and touched it to the powder hole in one of
the guns. This was done at the order of General Eliott,
who at the same time ordered the garrison band to
play "Britons Strike Home."

This first major bombardment continued all day.
It continued off and on day and night for years to
come, for Gibraltar's 14th siege was to last nearly as
long as all of the 13 earlier sieges put together. The
sound of the almost constant firing of Gibraltar's siege
guns and the sight of British battle flags flying from
the beleaguered fortress were to become a normal part
of life to the crews of ships sailing through the Straits.
In time, few sailors could recall what it was like passing
this way before the Great Siege had begun. Thus the
"Gibraltar tradition" continued to grow.

6. FAMINE ON THE ROCK

The Spanish gun batteries did not immediately respond to the bombardment from the Rock. In fact, the fortress was not directly attacked or shelled for 22 months after the siege began. The Spaniards and their French allies did not believe the British on Gibraltar could be defeated by gunfire — they would have to be starved out. With the land exit to the north cut off by thousands of enemy troops on the isthmus and the harbor blockaded by the powerful French-Spanish fleet, famine soon faced the Gibraltar garrison.

When the siege opened there were only about 40

The Great Siege—from an old print in the Gibraltar Museum
GIBRALTAR MUSEUM

head of cattle on the Rock. These were soon killed and eaten. Dogs were also destroyed. Since General Eliott was a vegetarian, going without meat did not bother him. As other supplies also began to run low, Eliott decided to conduct a test to see how little food he could live on. He managed to live and work on four ounces of rice a day for eight days. Within six months everyone in the garrison, soldiers and civilians alike, were living on an almost equally severe diet.

Unfortunately, some of the merchants who had hoarded supplies took advantage of the situation and charged huge prices for food. There was also some stealing, but Eliott dealt harshly with this. One soldier was publicly hanged after he was caught robbing a wineshop.

Eliott also found he had to provide armed guards with fixed bayonets to accompany bakers delivering bread. Even bread crumbs were carefully gathered and sold by the pound to those who could afford them. In time, no bread at all was available. What rice remained was so filled with weevils, one soldier reported, that it "looked like a plum pudding."

Weeds, dandelions and wild onions were gathered by civilian and military housewives to supplement family meals. In those days, the wife and children of a soldier often lived right on the army post to which the soldier was assigned, even in combat areas. This sometimes meant that from a strict military viewpoint women and children became useless mouths to feed. Such was the case at Gibraltar where every soldier, no matter how many members there were in his family, drew the same rations. To remedy this situation General Eliott ordered many military as well as civilian dependents evacuated from the Rock and sent to Malaga. Many, however, insisted that they be allowed to remain.

On January 15, 1780, after more than seven months of siege, a British brig managed to make its way through the cordon of Spanish and French warships blockading the Rock. The brig's captain and crew brought good news. The British Admiral, Sir George Rodney, and a convoy of ships carrying supplies and reinforcements were on their way to relieve Gibraltar. Off Cape St. Vincent, Rodney's escort vessels had encountered a powerful Spanish fleet and soundly defeated the enemy in a night battle. Rodney had not only captured a number of Spanish provision ships, but he also had captured the enemy commander, Admiral Don Juan de Langara.

As Rodney and his warships approached Gibraltar, the enemy squadrons that had been blockading the Rock fell back beyond Algeciras. This allowed the British convoy to enter the harbor and begin unloading troops and supplies. One of the first persons ashore was the captured Admiral Langara, who was taken to see General Eliott. Langara was astonished to learn that the midshipman in charge of the rowboat that brought him ashore was Prince William, the 15-year-old sailor son of Britain's King George. Langara could not imagine a member of any country's royal family performing such lowly chores.

Prince William continued to serve with the Royal

Navy for several years, and when he was crowned
King William IV he was often called "The Sailor King,"
a title of which he was particularly proud. While he
was at Gibraltar he was shown about the fortifications
by the officer of engineers, Lieutenant Colonel William
Green. When Prince William returned to England he
brought his father a map of Gibraltar that he had
drawn under Green's guidance.

In mid-February, 1780, Admiral Rodney and most
of his war fleet sailed for the West Indies. As soon
as they were out of sight, the French-Spanish squadrons resumed their blockade of the Rock. Battle
casualties were few but disease, mainly scurvy, soon
began to take its toll. When the scurvy — a diet-
deficiency disease — was at its height, a Danish ship
loaded with lemons got lost in a fog, drifted near the
Rock and was captured. It had only recently been
discovered that fresh lemons or limes were a cure for
scurvy. General Eliott ordered that lemon juice be
mixed with rum and issued to the garrison. Temporarily, at least, his men were rid of scurvy, but disease
continued to plague the Rock and its defenders
throughout the siege.

In the spring the enemy — who was also suffering
severely from disease — tried a novel method of
breaching the Gibraltar defenses from its seaward side.
This was an attempt, by the use of fire ships, to
destroy the few remaining British vessels anchored
near the New Mole.

On a dark and cloudy night early in June, the

crew members of the British ship *Enterprise* were
suddenly aware of three ships silently bearing down
on them. The crew challenged the oncoming ships and,
when no answer was received, warning shots were
fired across their bows. Suddenly the mysterious on-
rushing vessels burst into flames from waterline to
masthead.

The gunners aboard the *Enterprise* poured volley
after volley of cannon shells into the fire ships. This
cannonade alerted gunners on the Rock, and shells
from the shore batteries also began to explode on the
decks of the flaming enemy vessels.

Cannon shells alone were not enough to drive off
the fire ships. Crews from all the British vessels in the
harbor manned their small boats and succeeded in
getting grappling hooks and lines aboard the fire
ships. They were then towed out of the harbor and
allowed to drift out to sea.

The attack by the fire ships very nearly succeeded.
There were nine of these vessels in all, and the first
three came within a few yards of smashing into the
Enterprise and setting it ablaze. Had the *Enterprise*
gone up in flames the chances were good that her sister
warship, *Panther,* as well as 20 smaller vessels, would
also have been destroyed. In addition, the New Mole
itself was seriously threatened.

Fire ships had been used before in warfare.
Usually, however, their holds were filled with gunpowder so that when they rammed an enemy or were
struck by cannon fire they exploded and destroyed

nearby ships or docks. The fire ships used against
Gibraltar had no gunpowder in their holds. They had
simply been coated with tar and oil, set afire by their
crews and then abandoned to sail freely with the wind
into the anchored British vessels.

One other novel method of warfare was used at
Gibraltar during the Great Siege. A British Captain,
John Mercier, developed a method of firing mortar
shells into the Spanish lines and timing the shells'
flight so that they would explode in the air over the
heads of the enemy. Twenty years later an officer in
the Royal Artillery, Henry Shrapnel, perfected the
Gibraltar-type fragmentation shell that has since been
called by his name.

The development of the balloon was also given
strong impetus by the Great Siege. In June, 1783,
the French Montgolfier brothers, Joseph· and Etienne,
sent aloft to a height of several thousand feet a huge
paper bag filled with hot air from a straw fire.

Afterwards, the Montgolfier brothers said the
development of their balloon had been inspired by an
engraving they had seen of the French and Spanish
besieging the Rock. The sheer cliffs of the Rock
appeared to be impossible to ascend, but in a balloon
the attackers could rise above the fortress and then
descend upon it. No such device was ever used at
Gibraltar, of course, but in the American Civil War
and in World War I the balloon did prove to have
important military uses — mainly for observation purposes.

With the failure of the fire ships to breach the Gibraltar defenses, an iron blockade was once again clamped down on the Rock. Now disease began to take a truly serious toll. Smallpox struck the garrison, killing more than 500 people. Few of the victims were soldiers, but the families of soldiers and civilians were hard hit, as many as 20 children a week dying for some months. Food shortages again began to appear, adding to the defenders' burden.

In the spring of 1781, just when food, ammunition and morale were at their lowest ebb, the siege was again lifted — this time by a relief convoy from Britain under the command of Vice Admiral George Darby. The 100 supply ships were protected by 33 men-of-war. The Spanish fleet made no attempt to stop this formidable array of warships, but upon their approach to Gibraltar the fortress and the British ships came under a storm of fire from a number of Spanish gunboats as well as from the French-Spanish shore batteries. The enemy had chosen just this moment to begin his long-withheld bombardment of the Rock.

On the whole, Darby's convoy suffered little damage and most of the supplies were landed, but only under the greatest difficulty. For more than a week soldiers, sailors and civilians worked twenty-four hours a day under a steady rain of shot and shell. Despite the bombardment, the last stores were landed by the end of April, and Admiral Darby sailed for home.

Once again Gibraltar's supplies had been replenished, and 700 infantrymen had been added to the

garrison, but now the defenders faced an almost con-
tinuous artillery bombardment. Within a few weeks
every building in the town lay in ruins. At the peak of
their activity enemy guns fired 10,000 rounds of shot
and shell during one twenty-four-hour period. During
one six-week period more than 75,000 rounds of shot
and shell were fired into the fortress.

General Eliott, Colonel Green and their aides had
constructed the Rock's fortifications so well that the
military defenders suffered few battle casualties, but
the civilians in the shattered town did not fare so well.
The cannonade from the northern isthmus caused
many of the civilians to move to an encampment at
the southern tip of the Rock, but here they were at
the mercy of the small but deadly Spanish gunboats.
One mother wrote the following account of her ex-
periences at this time:

"A woman whose tent was a little below mine
was cut in two as she was drawing on her stockings.
Our servant made a kind of breastwork of beds,
trunks, mattresses, bolsters, and whatever else he could
find, and set me behind them. The balls fell around
me on every side. Every time the gunboats came I
dragged my poor children out of bed and hid with
them behind a rock. The third night I was here a ball
struck the rock and covered us with dirt and stones.
In a few minutes a shell burst so near me I had
scarcely time to run out of the way."

Gradually, as the summer wore on, the bombardment slackened. At this point, however, Eliott was

aware of a new threat, and he planned a bold stroke against it. Month by month the enemy's lines had been moved closer and closer to the foot of the Rock, and Eliott suspected that the bombardment had been intended as the prelude to an enemy attempt to storm the fortress. Eliott's plan was to mount a night attack against the enemy's advance positions. He realized that in sending a raiding party outside the fortress he ran a grave risk of not only losing some of his infantrymen but also of having the walls of the fortress facing on the isthmus breached by an enemy counterattack. But it was a gamble he felt he must take.

7. OPERATION STEADY

One of the things that made General Eliott an out-
standing commanding officer was his ability to judge
leadership qualities in the men who served under him.
This was dramatically illustrated when he chose the
leader of the attack against the Spanish forward lines
in late November, 1781.

The attack outside the fortress walls was called a
sortie. The password for the great sortie was "Steady."
All the members of the garrison, and especially Deputy
Governor Robert Boyd, were taken completely by
surprise when General Eliott placed Brigadier General

Charles Ross in direct command of Operation Steady.

Ross was a difficult, headstrong officer who had been in trouble of various kinds since the Great Siege had begun. Most of this trouble centered around Ross's intense and open dislike for General Boyd. The two high-ranking officers had frequently quarreled in front of their troops, but Eliott had ignored the incidents. He felt that strong-willed men confined to a small area like Gibraltar for a long period of time were likely to get on each other's nerves. Finally, however, Ross had insulted Boyd by calling him rude names and questioning his authority.

Ross was court-martialed, found guilty, sentenced to a year's suspension from duty and denied the right ever to serve again with his infantry regiment, the 39th. As Governor, General Eliott reviewed the court's findings. He cut the suspension to three months and refused to approve the latter part of the sentence. General Ross was now to have the opportunity to live up to General Eliott's faith in him.

Eliott's other great abilities as a military commander were demonstrated in the precision with which he worked out the plans for Operation Steady and the faultless way in which his well-trained men carried out the plans for one of the most difficult of all infantry operations – a night attack against entrenched positions.

Secrecy had always been one of the greatest problems at Gibraltar. In the siege of 1727, two men inside the fortress had been found guilty of planning to open the gates to the enemy. Brigadier General Clayton, who was then the Commandant, had ordered the traitors executed and their skins nailed to one of the Gibraltar gates as a future warning to spies. Eliott had no desire to take such harsh measures, but neither did he want the Spanish to know of his plans. Consequently, he did not alert his troops until the very last minute.

On the wild and stormy evening of November 26, General Eliott suddenly ordered 2,200 of his troops to assemble at midnight in an area called the Red Sands at the foot of the Rock. The assault forces represented almost half the soldiers in the garrison who were fit for duty. (More than 600 men were in the hospital recovering from illness or wounds.)

Eliott had already outlined the plan for the attack to General Ross and his aides, and they now quickly gave the necessary details to their men. At 2 A.M. on the rain-swept morning of November 27, 1781, three columns of infantry marched silently out of the north, or Landport, gate of the fortress toward the enemy lines.

Until now the area of sandy isthmus that stretched from the foot of the Rock to the Spanish forward lines had been regarded as a no man's land. Anyone on either side attempting to cross it was quickly spotted and shot. Eliott had chosen to launch his attack on just such a moonless and stormy night as this to avoid detection. Nevertheless, Ross's columns had not gone far before they were spotted by Spanish guards who fired warning shots and fled.

Expecting the enemy to open fire at any moment, Ross and his men moved resolutely forward. Instead of opening fire, however, the Spanish soldiers in the forward positions ran for their lives. Many did not run soon enough and were either shot or bayoneted by the British. The only indication of resistance was shown by about 40 Spanish cavalrymen, but as soon as they saw how badly outnumbered they were they turned and ran, as Eliott later reported, "as fast as their horses' legs could carry them."

As soon as they reached the enemy's front lines, the attackers went quickly to work spiking the big guns, blowing up ammunition and powder stores and setting fire to the fortifications in front of the trenches and around the main gun batteries. In later wars sandbags would be used to fortify trenches and gun positions, but at this time bundles of sticks called *fascines* were used. These could be set on fire easily, and they burned long and fiercely.

General Eliott had originally planned to remain inside the fortress during the attack, but at the last minute he could not resist joining his men. He, like all of his high-spirited troops, was itching for a fight after having been cooped up on the Rock for more than two years. Now, as the bundles of faggots surrounding the batteries went up in flames that were to burn for several days, Eliott shouted, "Look, men, how beautiful the Rock appears by the light of our glorious fires!"

The troops responded with a great burst of cheers and then started back toward the fortress. They were back inside the Landport gate before the Spanish guns began to bombard their own forward positions, futilely hoping to catch the British in the open. The entire attack had lasted slightly more than an hour, but the British had so effectively destroyed the enemy forward positions that it took months to repair them. Spanish losses in killed and wounded were never reported. British losses amounted to four men killed and 25 wounded. Ross and his men brought back a dozen prisoners and a report by the Spanish officer commanding the enemy guard — a report written somewhat too soon on this eventful evening. It read, "On this night nothing extraordinary happened."

All of the British Tommies — true to age-old soldiers' tradition — saw to it that they did not return to the fortress empty-handed. They brought back with them vegetables — mainly cabbages and cauliflower — that had been growing undisturbed in the no man's land, where everyone had been afraid to venture to pick them.

In the Garrison Orders for November 27, 1781, General Eliott wrote the following terse but meaningful statement: "The bravery and conduct of the whole detachment, officers and soldiers, on this glorious occasion surpasses the Governor's utmost acknowledgments." And below Eliott's statement the following words were written: "Brigadier General Charles Ross begs to thank the Governor for entrusting him with the command and desires to make a most public avowal of the firm and good behavior of the officers and men on this occasion." General Ross had indeed lived up to General Eliott's faith in him.

Despite the unqualified success of the night attack, General Eliott knew its effects would be only temporary. As soon as the enemy gun positions were restored, the bombardment of Gibraltar would again begin. This proved to be the case. By the early spring of 1782 enemy cannonballs began to rain down inside the fortress.

It was during this period of the siege that two teen-aged boys of the garrison helped prevent a number of British soldiers from becoming casualties. These boys had such keen eyesight that they could see the slow-moving cannonballs — as compared with the speed of modern artillery shells — while they were still in flight!

Each morning at dawn young John Brand, who was nicknamed "Shot" by the soldiers, and his friend Tom Richmond, called "Shell," took their lookout posts atop the fortress walls and scanned the skies toward Spain. When they saw cannonballs headed toward the fortress, they sounded an alarm, and the British soldiers ran for cover inside the stone casements.

As the bombardment continued, General Eliott was not idle. He was experimenting with a new weapon that he believed would successfully repel any future assault on the fortress. That another attack was coming — and a major one — Eliott was certain. He not only could see many signs of enemy preparation, but the few dispatches that blockade runners brought him from London also warned him of the onslaught that was being planned. It was becoming more and more clear, in fact, that most of the nations of the world were expecting the British to lose Gibraltar just as they had recently lost the war of the American Revolution.

General Eliott never even considered defeat. As the Spanish and French went about their preparations for a new attack, Eliott and his aides went about their preparations with their new weapon. If this new weapon was as successful as Eliott was certain it would be, the siege would come to an end — and it would end in British victory.

8. THE RED-HOT SHOT
OF GIBRALTAR

With the surrender of Lord Charles Cornwallis to
General George Washington at Yorktown on October
19, 1781, the British admitted the loss of their American colonies. The additional loss of Gibraltar in
Europe would be a blow from which Great Britain
might not recover her position as a world power.

Spain, aided by a powerful French fleet and a
large army under the French Duke of Crillon, now
decided to make one final, all-out effort to recapture
the Rock. The other nations of the world watched and
waited, wondering when the final blow would fall on
the beleaguered British garrison.

Because the British defense of Gibraltar had been so stubborn, the Spanish offered rewards throughout Europe for plans to subdue the fortress. A French military engineer, Michaud d'Arçon, suggested an ingenious scheme for building a number of unsinkable, shellproof, fireproof vessels. Ten of these so-called battering ships were built. Actually they were armored floating gun batteries, mounting a total of more than 200 new brass cannon and clad on their fighting sides — the sides that would face Gibraltar — with several layers of green timber, cork, iron and animal hides. Inside the hulls were beds of wet sand, and elaborate systems of pipes circulated water throughout the ships to prevent fires from spreading. In addition, to protect the crews, the vessels were covered with slanting, shellproof roofs from which cannonballs would roll harmlessly into the sea.

The engineer d'Arçon also designed landing ramps for the battering vessels. These ramps were hinged so they could be lowered for troops to walk on in case an amphibious landing was possible. They were not unlike the ramps on modern military infantry and vehicle landing craft.

In addition to the 10 battering ships, the combined French-Spanish fleet numbered 47 ships of the line. These included seven three-deck men-of-war, 31 two-deck warships, several frigates and a number of smaller vessels.

On the land side, the Duke of Crillon's forces numbered upwards of 40,000 men. Their heavy gun batteries included about 250 cannons and mortars as against the less than 100 that the 6,000 Gibraltar defenders commanded. These outnumbered Gibraltar guns and their gallant crews, however, were what would decide the final issue.

Preparations for the French-Spanish assault went on for months. People throughout Europe talked about the coming battle, and many made plans to go and watch it. As they prepared for the attack, the enemy did not let up on his bombardment of the Rock. In fact it was so seldom that a day passed without shells landing inside the fortress that it was noted in garrison records and diaries. In the spring of 1782, the bombardment suddenly became more severe and the British thought the attack was about to begin. But the enemy gunfire slackened and the watching and waiting again began.

Meanwhile, General Eliott and his men went about making their own preparations for the defense of the Rock. With the aid of his deputy, General Boyd, further experiments were carried on with Eliott's new war weapon — special kinds of cannonballs to be fired at the enemy warships as well as at the French-Spanish land fortifications.

Eliott also tried to figure out some way to place his heavy guns so they could fire more effectively at the French-Spanish troops. One day, as he and some of his men stood near the top of the Rock, Eliott said: "You know, I'd give a thousand pounds to anyone who could suggest a way to put our guns in a spot where they could fire directly at the enemy."

This gave Sergeant Major Henry Ince, who was

standing with his commanding officer, Colonel Green,
a chance to suggest something he had been thinking
about for some time.

"General Eliott, sir," Sergeant Ince said, "why
don't we blast a tunnel from this point right through
the Rock to the other side? At the point where the
tunnel comes out we can place a gun battery that will
be looking right down the throats of the enemy."

Eliott thought the idea was so good that he put
Sergeant Ince to work immediately. On May 25, 1782,
Ince and his men started the first — but far from the
last — tunnel or gallery through the Rock. It was six
feet high and six feet wide and to reach the other
side of the Rock it would have to extend 200 feet
through solid limestone.

A small, wiry man, Sergeant Ince was a regular
army soldier who was known for his ambition and love
of hard work. He drove his men relentlessly. They had
not gone very far, however, before the clouds of rock
dust stirred up by their blasting with gunpowder and
hammering with hand tools made it almost impossible
to breathe in the tunnel. They decided to blast a hole
through the side of the tunnel for ventilation. As soon
as they did so, it became apparent that this opening
along the face of the Rock would itself make an excellent spot for mounting a large cannon.

Meanwhile, General Eliott had sent an urgent
message to England asking for miners to assist in
blasting out the galleries. Soon blockade runners
landed the miners on Gibraltar and other tunnels

besides Sergeant Ince's were begun. By early fall, several galleries had been blasted out of the solid limestone, and a half-dozen gun batteries were in place. The enemy's fortifications had been made almost useless by this bold stroke, since from such a great height the newly placed Gibraltar guns could fire right down on the unprotected heads of the French and Spanish troops on the isthmus.

Early in September, civilian spectators began to gather on the nearby high points of land that provided the best view of the Rock and the Bay and Strait of Gibraltar. By September 13, 1782, the day on which the final grand assault of the Great Siege began, there were upwards of 100,000 men, women and children gathered like fans at a sports contest to view the coming battle. It was to be a sight worth watching, for as one witness later wrote, "It was a military spectacle such as the annals of war had never before presented."

The first enemy ships to move into firing positions were the 10 armored floating batteries. These formidable vessels moved to within half a mile of the western sea face of the Rock and began to pour a fury of shot and shell into the fortress and town. The Gibraltar gunners were at first pleased at how close inshore the battering ships had moved, because at such short range they presented excellent targets. It soon became clear, however, that the heaviest cold shot and shell from the garrison guns simply rolled off the shellproof roofs of the armored ships.

The enemy men-of-war, meanwhile, moved into

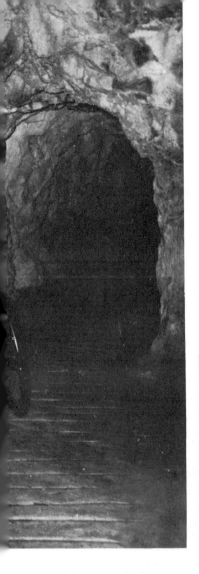

An early cannon
—C. MONTEGRIFFO

INCE'S GALLERY
DURING THE GREAT SIEGE, 1779-1782,
WHEN THE SPANISH LINES APPROACHED
SO CLOSE TO THE ROCK THAT IT WAS
IMPOSSIBLE TO FIRE DOWN UPON THEM,
THE GOVERNOR OFFERED A REWARD TO
ANYONE WHO COULD GET A GUN ON TO
THE PROJECTION KNOWN AS THE NOTCH.
SERGEANT MAJOR INCE OF THE CORPS
OF MILITARY ARTIFICERS, SUGGESTED
TUNNELING AND WORK STARTED HERE
ON MAY 25TH, 1782.

position 1,200 yards offshore and their heavy guns as well as those from the French-Spanish land batteries began to lend their weight to the bombardment. This fierce cannonade was to continue without respite for some eight hours.

The attack was not many hours old before General Eliott ordered his gunners to begin using the new weapon he had developed — the red-hot shot that was to become famous after this day's fighting. These were cannonballs that had been heated in furnaces and then quickly loaded into large guns and fired at the enemy.

The problem with the red-hot shot was to prevent the cannons themselves from exploding when the heated cannonballs, or "roast potatoes" as the gunners called them, were placed next to the powder in the guns. General Eliott had solved this problem by having his gunners ram a thick layer of water-soaked rags down the bore of each gun to separate the hot shot from the gunpowder. In early experiments some guns had exploded, killing several artillerymen. Other gunners had been severely burned in transferring the hot cannonballs from the furnaces to the guns by means of tongs. But continued drill had taught the gunners how to use their new weapon with minimum risk to themselves while inflicting maximum damage on the enemy.

Part of the delay in bringing the red-hot shot into action was caused by the fact that it took at least two hours to fire the furnaces and heat the cannonballs to a fiery glow. Once they went into action they began to take a telling effect.

At first, only wisps of smoke could be seen on the roofs of the armored floating batteries. But the Gibraltar gunners could see that their red-hot shot was not rolling off the vessels' slanted roofs as the cold shot had done. Fires began to break out on most of the battering ships, and General Eliott ordered several of his gun batteries to fire the hot cannonballs at the enemy warships in the bay and at the land fortifications on the isthmus.

By nightfall all the enemy's armored battering ships, as well as several men-of-war, were ablaze and several flaming frigates were trying to retreat. On the land side, the red-hot shot of Gibraltar also had begun to take its toll, causing such havoc that the enemy cannonade had fallen away to a few sporadic shots every hour.

As the evening came on, it became increasingly clear that the final French-Spanish attempt to seize the Rock would end in grim failure. It was at this point that Captain Roger Curtis of the Royal Navy performed a feat of courage and compassion that was above and beyond the call of duty. Taking command of 12 British gunboats, Curtis set out from the New Mole to rescue the crews of the enemy's 10 blazing battering ships.

To get to the stricken vessels Curtis and his men had to fight their way past several Spanish frigates. With their 18- and 24-pounder guns blazing away, Curtis's squadron of rescue boats headed right at the Spanish warships. Since Curtis's small boats' guns were leveled at the enemy warships' waterline, they could inflict lethal damage with little fear of immediate retaliation, and the Spanish frigates hastily retreated. Behind them, they left the flaming battering ships with hundreds of helpless men aboard.

"At the risk of his own life and the lives of his crew members who were equally daring," General Eliott later wrote in dispatches to the Admiralty, "Curtis took his gunboats right alongside the sinking enemy vessels and began rescuing the wounded, burned, and dying enemy from the flaming derelicts." At one point Curtis and his crew were alongside a ship as it blew up, killing one member of Curtis's command and wounding several others.

Despite such dangers, Curtis and his heroic gunboat crews continued their rescue efforts. Curtis himself helped many of the enemy from the blazing decks of the floating batteries to his gunboat. At the loss of a single British gunboat more than 350 of the enemy sailors were thus saved.

At dawn on September 14, the Bay of Gibraltar presented a pitiful picture of the wreckage of the French-Spanish assault fleet. Hulks of burning ships were to be seen everywhere. Men clung to some of these still-flaming wrecks. Following Captain Curtis's example, the Gibraltar artillerymen ceased their bombardment and, temporarily leaving their guns, took to small boats and attempted to rescue the enemy survivors.

Enemy warships that were still afloat were already retreating toward the coast of Africa that was barely visible through the faint light of early dawn and the gunsmoke that partly obscured the Straits. On the land side, fortifications also blazed, and in the early-morning light, crews of enemy infantrymen could be seen trying to extinguish the flames so that they could continue their bombardment.

Actually the bombardment from the isthmus and the Spanish mainland did continue, if only in sporadic fashion, through most of the next day, since it took the troops on the northern side of the Rock some time to realize the disaster that had befallen the grand assault from the sea.

As awareness of the defeat of the sea assault began to spread there was talk among the leaders of the French-Spanish land forces about attempting an infantry attack across the no man's land of the isthmus. The Duke of Crillon, however, talked his aides out of such a suicidal venture. A veteran of numerous European campaigns, the Duke realized that however well the siege campaign might have been planned, it had been utterly defeated by General Eliott's red-hot shot from Gibraltar.

During the course of the action on September 13 and 14, the Gibraltar garrison had fired 8,300 rounds of red-hot shot from their guns and used 716 barrels of gunpowder. The French-Spanish land and sea forces fired 30,000 rounds of cold shot and shell. Enemy casualties were more than 2,000 men, with almost 1,500 killed, wounded, or missing among the crews of the floating batteries alone. Losses among the Gib-

Moorish castle—C. MONTEGRIFFO

raltar garrison were relatively light, with one officer and 15 men killed and five officers and 63 men wounded.

Throughout Spain and France news of the failure of the attack was received with despair and disbelief. The thousands of spectators who had gathered in expectation of witnessing the fall of Gibraltar returned to their homes utterly dejected.

In England, of course, there was great rejoicing. The news of the lifting of the Great Siege brought new hope to the hearts of the British people who had suffered through the disaster of the American Revolution and knew that complete decline of the British Empire would have followed on the heels of the loss of Gibraltar. But the Rock itself had not only proved to be invulnerable — it became a full-blown symbol of the invulnerability of the British Empire.

The Great Siege did not officially end until September 3, 1783, with the signing of a treaty at Versailles in France. It confirmed the Treaty of Utrecht between Spain and Great Britain. Long before that date, however, the enemy guns had ceased to threaten the Rock and there was no longer any need for the British lion to roar its defiance from Gibraltar.

For a time after the final assault, the Spaniards continued to bombard the fortress, firing more than 1,200 rounds a day during the rest of September. Early in October, however, a British fleet consisting of 34 ships of the line, 6 frigates and 31 cargo ships under Admiral Richard Howe relieved the Rock, landing hundreds of tons of ammunition and supplies and reinforcements of 1,600 men.

At the end of October, the enemy land forces began to break camp and within a few weeks the Great Siege had to all apparent purposes ended. During the entire siege, 333 men of the garrison had been killed, 536 had died from sickness (mainly scurvy), and 319 were discharged because of wounds or "incurable complaints." And 872 officers and men had been wounded but returned to duty.

The Spaniards claimed to have lost 6,000 men, but it is generally agreed that their losses were much greater.

The British fired 205,328 rounds of ammunition and used up 8,000 barrels of gunpowder during the Great Siege. The enemy fired 258,387 rounds of shot and shell.

The Great Siege officially lasted 3 years, 7 months, and 12 days.

At the end of the Great Siege, the Duke of Crillon paid an official courtesy visit to the Rock, where he was the guest of General Eliott. The Duke was especially impressed with the galleries that had been started by Sergeant Ince and extended for 500 to 600 feet within the Rock. Sergeant Ince was not especially flattered to hear the Duke exclaim, upon seeing the galleries hewn out of solid limestone, "These works are worthy of the Romans!" After all Sergeant Ince's Celtic ancestors had driven the Romans out of Britain!

To General Eliott the Duke said, "I'd rather see

you and your artillerymen here and shake your hands as friends than face you as enemies at your gun batteries where you never spared me!"

Although General Eliott was 65 years old when the Great Siege ended, he remained as Governor of the Rock for four more years. When he reached England in 1787, he was raised to the peerage and given the title of Lord Heathfield, Baron of Gibraltar. He had already been awarded the Order of the Bath and a pension of 1,500 pounds a year during special ceremonies on the Rock. In 1788 Eliott suffered a stroke and died a short time later. Eliott had requested that he be buried among his fallen comrades at Gibraltar, but he was buried at his home at Heathfield in Sussex.

General Robert Boyd, Eliott's Deputy Governor at Gibraltar, succeeded to the Governorship of the Rock in 1790. He died four years later and was buried at Gibraltar.

Sergeant Major Henry Ince lived on the Rock for many years, following his retirement from the British army after 30 years' service. His farm home there still bears his name, as do other landmarks. Extremely active in community affairs, Ince was one of the founders of a church in Gibraltar whose first meeting had been held in his home in 1769. Near the end of his life he returned to England. He died at Penzance in 1809 at the age of 72.

All the surviving members of the military garrison who served on Gibraltar during the Great Siege were

THE ARMS OF GIBRALTAR

MONTIS·INSIGNIA·CALPE

honored by being granted the Castle and Key insignia bearing the motto, "Montis Insignia Calpe," which was the ancient coat of arms or insignia for Gibraltar; Montis meaning mountain and Calpe being the Pillar of Hercules on the European continent.

Three German regiments who served with the British garrison, as well as their descendants, were granted permission to wear the word "Gibraltar" as a shoulder patch. Long years later, British Tommies in World War I were occasionally startled to capture German prisoners who proudly displayed the "Gibraltar" shoulder patch on their uniforms! During World War II, Adolf Hitler finally got around to abolishing the honorary British "Gibraltar" badges among the Reichswehr troops.

Between the end of the Great Siege and the beginning of World War I, the great limestone Rock of Gibraltar continued to occupy center stage in numerous battle dramas. One of the most important of these took place in 1805 during the Napoleonic Wars, when Britain's Admiral Horatio Nelson defeated the combined French and Spanish fleets in one of the key naval battles in the history of the world. The battle was fought off Cape Trafalgar at the western entrance to the Straits of Gibraltar.

9. THE BATTLE OF
TRAFALGAR

For ten years after the Great Siege ended in 1783, life
at Gibraltar was relatively peaceful. Then Napoleon
Bonaparte proclaimed himself Emperor in France, and
his armies, like those of the German Dictator Adolf
Hitler almost a century-and-a-half later, began to over-
run Europe.

During the first part of this conflict, Spain sided
with Britain against France, and the Rock served
mainly as a naval base for British and Spanish warships. But then, after a brief period of peace in 1802-3,
fighting was resumed, and once again the Rock was

threatened — for this time Spain sided with the French against their old enemies, the British. The second part of this general European conflict was known as the Napoleonic Wars after the self-proclaimed French Emperor.

There was a strong and curious resemblance between Napoleon and Hitler and the wartime paths along which they led their respective nations, first to great military glory and finally to dismal defeat. Napoleon was called the "Little Corporal" and Hitler was a corporal in World War I. Both men regarded themselves as military geniuses, although in Napoleon's case the claim was closer to the truth. Both dictators dreamed of governing world empires, and both men's dreams ended in ashes. Napoleon died alone in 1821 on the tiny island of St. Helena, where he had been exiled six years earlier. Hitler committed suicide in Berlin in 1945, near the end of World War II.

There were other parallels in the two dictators' paths of war. On his way to world conquest Napoleon sent his armies into Egypt, where they were defeated by the British. Hitler's armies overran the Middle East but were driven out of Africa and back along the road to defeat following the combined British-American Operation Torch in 1942. The armies of both Napoleon and Hitler were smashed in winter campaigns against Russia — Napoleon's attack against Moscow and Hitler's attack against Stalingrad both ending in disaster.

Finally, both men made serious plans to invade England, and in both instances England alone stood

in the way of a military dictator gaining complete
control of Western Europe. In 1940 it was the Royal
Air Force that challenged the German *Luftwaffe* in
its attempt to pave the way for the invasion of
England by Hitler's hordes.

During the second week of September, 1940, as
Great Britain waited for the peak of the German
aerial onslaught, Prime Minister Winston Churchill
made a radio speech to his people in which he told
them they must regard the next few days as perhaps
the most important period in their nation's history. "It

Trafalgar Cemetery—C. MONTEGRIFFO

ranks," Churchill said, "with the days when Nelson stood between us and Napoleon's Grand Army at Boulogne."

The Royal Air Force, of course, defeated the German *Luftwaffe* in the now legendary Battle of Britain, thus ending the Hitler invasion plan that was known as Operation Sea Lion.

Toward the end of 1805, the period to which Churchill referred in his radio speech, both Gibraltar and Great Britain were expecting to be invaded at any moment. But the most immediate threat seemed to be aimed at England, for across the English Channel at Boulogne Napoleon had massed more than 100,000 troops.

His plan at first was to quickly launch an amphibious assault against the British Isles before the Royal Navy could react against his fast-moving assault craft. He soon realized, however, that such a move might well end in disaster, and that he must have complete control of the Channel before such an invasion could be launched. The man who stood in the way of Napoleon's navy was Britain's Admiral Horatio Nelson, one of the greatest sea fighters who ever lived.

Horatio Nelson had been a sailor since he was 12, when his uncle, Captain Maurice Suckling, took him on a voyage to the Falkland Islands, in the South Atlantic. A frail, sickly lad, Horatio had been born at Burnham-Thorpe in Norfolk on September 29, 1758. His father was a clergyman.

After his first voyage, young Nelson never lost his

love of the sea. At 15 he served as a coxswain on a ship that sailed to the Arctic. At 18 he became a lieutenant in the Royal Navy. Before he was 21 he was given command of his first ship, the frigate *Hinchin-brooke*.

Twice during these early years, Nelson was stricken with tropical fever, once after a voyage to the East Indies and a second time after a cruise to Central America. After both illnesses he was almost invalided out of the service, but he insisted upon returning to active duty.

When the prelude to the Napoleonic Wars broke out in 1793, Nelson was given command of the *Agamemnon*. Again and again during the course of the next decade, he distinguished himself in sea fights against the French fleet in the Mediterranean and elsewhere. At Calvi, however, on the coast of Corsica, he was wounded and lost the sight in his right eye. In 1797, in an engagement in the Canary Islands his right arm was shattered by gunfire and had to be amputated. This injury forced him to return to England for several months, but when he had only partly recovered he was back in action.

It was at this point that Napoleon was threatening to invade Egypt, and Nelson was given the responsibility of stopping Napoleon's invasion fleet. This Nelson did in a bold maneuver at Aboukir Bay, at the mouth of the Nile River. Nelson discovered the French fleet anchored in the small bay and remarked to one of his aides, "Where there's room for a French ship to anchor, there's room for a British ship to sail." He then ordered his men-of-war into the narrow passageway between the shore and the enemy ships and virtually destroyed the French squadron with a series of broadsides. The victory, called the Battle of the Nile, made Nelson's name a household word in England.

In 1801, Nelson was named a Vice Admiral and celebrated the promotion by taking part in an action in which the British defeated the Danish fleet at Copenhagen. During the course of this battle the commander of the British warships, Admiral Parker, hoisted a flag ordering his ships to retreat. Nelson, according to legend, raised a telescope to his blind eye and said to an aide, "I can't see the signal." He then led his ship into the thick of the fray and his example inspired the rest of the British captains to continue the fight, turning defeat into victory.

Shortly after this triumph, the City of London prepared to honor Nelson at a special ceremony, but Nelson refused to take part in the affair because the rest of the men in his command had not been invited. "Not until London thinks justly of the merits of my brave companions," Nelson said, "can I receive any special attention."

In the spring of 1803, Admiral Nelson was given command of the British Mediterranean squadrons with orders to seek and destroy the French war fleet. There then began a two-year game of hare and hounds in which Nelson aboard his flagship, the *Victory*, and the men-of-war under his command tried to bring the enemy warships to bay. A part of this game of hare and hounds was an attempt on the part of Napoleon's navy to draw the British ships away from the English Channel so that the British Isles would be unprotected from Napoleon's planned invasion.

For a year-and-a-half Nelson succeeded in bottling up the enemy fleet in the harbor at Toulon. During this period, Gibraltar and Malta were used as British supply bases. Finally, the enemy squadrons managed to slip out of Toulon harbor, and Nelson chased them all the way to the West Indies and back again. This time the quarry escaped into the harbor at Cadiz north of the Cape of Trafalgar, where they were joined by half-a-dozen Spanish men-of-war. This combined enemy fleet was kept under close observation by several British warships under Admiral Sir Cuthbert Collingwood.

On his way back from the West Indies, Nelson had stopped at Gibraltar for much-needed supplies. This was the first time he had set foot on land for two years, although he had stopped at Gibraltar long enough on one previous occasion to leave his clothes to be laundered and to send a message to the Governor, General R. E. Fox, in which Nelson said, "I am particularly desirous to give comfort to the old Rock." Then he was off again in pursuit of the enemy.

This time he remained long enough to make certain that Gibraltar was in no serious danger. Spanish gunboats had been harassing British shipping in

Admiral Horatio Nelson—BRITISH NATIONAL MARITIME MUSEUM

the Straits, and there had been what seemed to be a growing threat from the land side, where 12,000 to 15,000 Spanish soldiers were encamped. But Nelson soon learned that the Spanish planned to make no immediate attempt upon the Rock. The truth of the matter was that while Spain was officially at war with England, the Spanish people themselves hated Napoleon and the French.

After leaving Gibraltar, Nelson returned briefly to England on leave. He had no sooner arrived at Merton in Surrey, when news reached the British Admiralty in London that the enemy combined fleet was gathering in great numbers at Cadiz. In reporting this, Admiral Collingwood said that the masts of the enemy looked like a great forest of trees. Admiral Nelson was immediately ordered to sea. He sailed from England in mid-September, 1805, with just three warships under his command. Admiral Collingwood, however, had already been reinforced with 22 British men-of-war. The French-Spanish combined fleet in the harbor at this time consisted of 33 ships, 15 of which were Spanish, under the command of the French Admiral Pierre de Villeneuve.

Nelson arrived off Cadiz on September 28, the day before his 47th birthday. For several weeks he made every effort to get the enemy to try to run the blockade of Cadiz Harbor, but the combined fleet refused to accept the challenge. Finally, Admiral de Villeneuve decided to try and make a run for it and escape into the Mediterranean. This was the chance Admiral Nelson had been waiting for.

The morning of October 21, 1805, dawned bright and clear but there was very little wind blowing. This, in a day of sailing ships, called for an immediate reassessment of the battle situation and a possible change in plans. Nelson directed the captains under him to reset their sails to take advantage of what breeze there was. He did not, however, call upon them to change their plans to engage the enemy as quickly and as directly as possible.

As the French-Spanish fleet set sail to leave Cadiz harbor and head for the western entrance to the Straits of Gibraltar, Nelson sent a message to all of the ships in his fleet: "If you lay your enemy close alongside," the message read, "you cannot go far wrong." That is, he expected them to run their ships close enough to the enemy so that they would be able, first, to fire point-blank broadsides of cannon, grapeshot, and musket fire, and, second, that they would board the enemy vessels and fight the enemy crews in cutlass-swinging hand-to-hand combat. (This order was not unlike those given to British front-line troops during World War I when they were sent over-the-top to engage the Germans in hand-to-hand combat.)

Then Nelson added the inspiring phrase that has continued to echo down the years and today is the motto of the Royal Navy, "England expects that every man will do his duty."

Villeneuve's combined French and Spanish fleet consisted of 33 warships, while the men-of-war under Nelson's command numbered only 27. Nevertheless Nelson attacked unhesitatingly. His strategy was simple but daring. The enemy ships were sailing single file in a straight line. Nelson sent the squadron under Admiral Collingwood in the *Royal Sovereign* directly at the straight line with orders to break through it and cut off the last 12 ships. Collingwood followed Nelson's orders, almost to the letter, except that he cut off the last 16 ships from the line. Nelson in the *Victory* sailed his squadron directly under the guns of the forward and center ships, the most powerful in the enemy battle line, to draw the fire away from Collingwood's squadron. Nelson's self-sacrificing action was the sort of effort that would have won him the Congressional Medal of Honor or the Navy Cross were he an American in today's fighting, or the Victoria Cross in modern British warfare.

Collingwood's and Nelson's bold attacks completely confused the enemy, who had been expecting a drawn-out battle of maneuver. Before the French and Spanish crews could recover, they were hit by devastating cannonades from the British men-of-war and found themselves face-to-face with the cutlass-swinging boarding parties. Within a few hours the French-Spanish fleet was destroyed, without the loss of a single British man-of-war.

But the British paid a heavy price, nevertheless. At the height of the conflict, while the *Victory* was locked in close battle with the *Rédoubtable,* an enemy sniper fired a musket shot from the latter ship's topmast that fatally wounded Admiral Nelson. He fell and was carried belowdecks by one of his men, Thomas

Hardy. Nelson, his life ebbing away, kept asking how the battle was going. Just before he died he was told that the battle was proving to be an overwhelming British success. "Thank God!" Nelson said, "I have done my duty."

When the smoke of battle cleared, the British had captured 19 or 20 enemy ships. They had also captured the enemy commander, Admiral de Ville-neuve. The combined fleet's warships were taken in tow by the British men-of-war, which set sail for Gibraltar, but within a few hours a storm blew up off Cape Trafalgar and the British fleet and its prizes were scattered across the seas. As a result of this storm and the battle damage, which caused a number of the enemy vessels to capsize and sink, only four enemy warships – one French and three Spanish – were towed into Gibraltar Harbor.

Despite the gale the British ships that were still seaworthy managed to resume their blockade of Cadiz. This greatly impressed the Spanish, who said, "How can you defeat such a people? The most violent of the elements seems to have no effect upon them."

Those British ships in need of repairs, plus the four enemy prize ships, limped into Rosia Harbor at Gibraltar on October 28. This tiny harbor – still in use today but mainly as a place where the local residents and tourists go swimming – would scarcely hold a modern cruiser or destroyer. Yet it could hold all of Britain's Mediterranean fleet plus its prizes after the Battle of Trafalgar.

Admiral Nelson's body was returned to Gibraltar in a cask of brandy lashed to the *Victory*'s mainmast (the alcohol acting as a preservative). According to one account, his body was taken ashore briefly when the *Victory* reached the Rock, but this has never been confirmed. It has been confirmed, however, that for the continued purpose of preservation Nelson's body was transferred from the cask of brandy to a cask of rum for the long voyage back to England, where the greatly loved victor of Trafalgar was buried in Westminster Abbey.

The *Victory* was badly damaged in the battle that cost Nelson his life and at first it was suggested that the Admiral's body be transferred to another ship for the long voyage home. This almost caused a mutiny aboard the *Victory*, whose crew insisted that they had brought Nelson out from Britain and they would return him there on his final voyage. Even wounded crew members insisted they be allowed to leave the hospital on the Rock so they could sail once more with Nelson. This was an almost unheard-of display of affection on the part of the seamen of the day, when life aboard a warship was brutally severe and discipline was merciless. Life aboard the *Victory* had been no different from that of any other ship of the line except for the radiant presence of Nelson, whose men worshipped him. His officers also regarded him highly, for he was one of the few naval commanders of the day who shared all of his plans with his aides. He believed that if his men knew the reasons for fighting a particular engagement and how that engagement would be fought, they would be more likely to fight harder and better than the enemy. This technique of commanding as well as Nelson's personal magnetism, never failed to inspire the men who served under him, and it was this inspiration that had brought about the overwhelming British victory in the Battle of Trafalgar.

Other British sailors and officers who were killed in the Battle of Trafalgar were buried at sea. The wounded who later died in the hospital at Gibraltar were buried on the Rock in a special cemetery near the Southport gate. These dead are honored to this day at an annual ceremony held at the small Trafalgar Cemetery.

Nelson's victory at Trafalgar was so decisive that it destroyed Spanish and French seapower and established Great Britain as undisputed mistress of the seas, but the Napoleonic Wars dragged on for almost a decade longer. The Peninsular War, which was an important part of the Napoleonic conflict, was fought on the Iberian peninsula between 1808 and 1814. During this period of the conflict, Spain changed sides and was an ally of the British and Portuguese against the French.

More than once during the seven campaigns of the Peninsular War, the Spanish were aided by their British allies on Gibraltar. This period represents one of the few times in the history of the Rock that the

Spanish and British governments were officially in agreement regarding the status of the Rock.

Napoleon was finally defeated by the combined armies of the British Duke of Wellington and the Prussian General Blücher in the campaign of Waterloo, in Belgium. On the Rock the victory of the "Iron Duke," as Wellington was called, over the "Corsican Monster," as Napoleon was called, was greeted with wild rejoicing and salutes fired from the main batteries of the fortress.

The friendship that had developed between the Gibraltarians and the Spanish during the Peninsular War grew and was strengthened during the rest of the 19th century and the beginning of the 20th century. Many British servicemen and their families vacationed in Spain and some built resort homes there. Many Spanish day workers came to Gibraltar to earn the excellent wages that prevailed there.

All during the rest of the 19th century, peace and prosperity reigned on the Rock. Much of the prosperity, which was unlike anything the Gibraltarians had ever known, was the direct result of the building of the Suez Canal by Britain's traditional enemy, the French.

10. "TRADE FOLLOWS THE FLAG"

When the Emperor Napoleon I was in Egypt during the Napoleonic Wars he directed one of his military engineers, J. M. Le Père, to make a study of the Isthmus of Suez (the neck of land that connects Africa and Asia). He wanted to know if it was possible to build a canal from the Mediterranean to the Gulf of Suez on the Red Sea. Such a canal, Napoleon knew, would make it possible to sail directly from the Mediterranean to the Indian Ocean, thus cutting off several thousand miles from the long trip around Africa by way of the Cape of Good Hope.

Le Père and his surveyors made a mistake in their calculations and concluded that the level of the Mediterranean was more than 30 feet below that of the Red Sea. This meant that a lockless canal could not be built, so the project was temporarily abandoned.

As the 19th century progressed and sailing vessels gradually gave way to steamships that could carry much more cargo at greater speeds than ever before, the need for a canal across the Suez isthmus continued to grow.* Finally, additional studies were made and it was discovered that it would indeed be possible to build a lockless, sea-level canal because there was actually little difference between the levels of the Mediterranean and the Red Sea.

Although no government officially backed the project, the French were mainly responsible for the Suez Canal's construction. Britain, despite the fact that she stood to gain more than any other nation from the canal, fought against it every step of the way. The English feared that the French would use the canal as a means to control Egypt and strangle traffic between Britain and Britain's prized possession, India.

The key figure in the construction of the Suez Canal was a French engineer and diplomat named Ferdinand de Lesseps. Years later he was to head a company that would fail and go bankrupt in its efforts to build the Panama Canal, but his efforts in building the Suez waterway were to meet with unqualified success.

* *The first steamship stopped at Gibraltar in 1823.*

De Lesseps was born at Versailles in 1805, the year Nelson won his victory at Trafalgar. When de Lesseps was 20 he went into the French consular and diplomatic service. He resigned from that service in 1849 and soon afterwards began to organize a company to build the Suez Canal.

Before de Lesseps entered the picture, much work had already been done on a canal across the Isthmus of Suez. This work had its beginnings long before the birth of Christ. The ancient Egyptians had actually dug a canal that connected the Nile River with the Red Sea, but it had not been maintained. In the 8th century A.D., it had fallen into complete disuse. Afterwards, there had been much speculation in Europe about the need for such a waterway, but it remained for de Lesseps to get the project under way.

During his diplomatic career, de Lesseps had served in Egypt and had become a friend of Mohammed Said Pasha (for whom Port Said was later named). When Said became the Viceroy of Egypt, de Lesseps told the new ruler his plan for the construction of a canal across the isthmus. Financing such a project was a major problem, but when de Lesseps explained his scheme for forming an international company to supply the needed funds, he immediately won the new Viceroy's approval. The French government, it was also made clear, would give its support to the proposed canal.

Few engineering problems were encountered in building the 100-mile-long canal. (The economic and political problems it created, however, have lived with the world until today.) Although it was about twice as long as the later Panama Canal, the Suez waterway was built across almost flat terrain, and there were no tropical-fever problems such as those encountered by the workmen in digging the "Big Ditch" in Panama.

The Suez project cost about $70 million, most of it subscribed by French private citizens and by members of the Ottoman, or Turkish, Empire that then controlled Egypt. The United States and Britain owned none of the original shares of Suez stock.

When the "big ditch in the sands" was officially opened on November 17, 1869, there were elaborate ceremonies at Port Said. A fleet of vessels from many nations steamed through the canal. The leading ship, a French yacht named *L'Aigle,* carried the Empress Eugenie, the wife of Napoleon III, who was the nephew of Napoleon I. Along the route all the ships stopped at the new palace of the Egyptian Viceroy for a state dinner and dedication ceremonies. At this official function 6,000 guests were entertained.

From a transportation standpoint, the Suez Canal was an instant success. Britain, with key Mediterranean strongholds at Gibraltar and the island of Malta, began to prosper from merchant-ship traffic through the Straits of Gibraltar and into the Mediterranean. Communications were also greatly improved. One of the first ships through the canal laid a cable, and direct communications with India were established in 1870.

Not long after the Suez Canal was opened, the new Egyptian Viceroy, Ismail Pasha, began to borrow large amounts of money from French and British banks. When he could not repay these loans, he sold Egypt's shares of stock in the Suez Canal to Britain's shrewd Prime Minister, Benjamin Disraeli. This was in 1875. A year later Ismail invited British and French government officials to supervise Egypt's finances. In 1882, Ismail's followers revolted, and the French withdrew from Egypt. Britain, however, sent in military forces, and Egypt became virtually a British dependency, despite the fact that it was still technically under the control of the Ottoman Empire.

Both Egypt and Britain prospered during the rest of the Victorian Age — named for Queen Victoria, who reigned in Britain from 1837 to 1901. During the Victorian Age there was tremendous industrial expansion in Britain and economic expansion abroad.

It was during this period that the Rock of Gibraltar fully emerged as the powerful symbol of the British Empire. The reason for Gibraltar's emergence as such a symbol was based on one factor: British Imperialism.

Imperialism — the exploitation of a foreign people and their country for the exploiter's gain — had been a way of life since the beginning of recorded history. The ancient Chinese, the Sumerians, the Egyptians, the Greeks and Romans had all expanded their empires by conquest. It was not until relatively modern times, however, that imperialism became what those who practiced it considered a practical necessity. This was caused by the Industrial Revolution.

The Industrial Revolution made it possible for all

European nations, and most especially England, to produce far more goods than they could sell in their own markets. Rapid transportation — the steamship and railroads — and shorter routes, such as that created by the Suez Canal, produced keen competition for foreign markets. Manufacturers seeking markets and businessmen seeking investments caused England to embark on a policy of modern imperialism. In this way, distant nations could be taken over and their trade controlled, and money could be invested to develop the conquered nations' natural resources.

Sometimes this aggressive expansion took the form of the outright annexation of a country in Africa or Asia. Occasionally it took the form of establishing a protectorate, that is the taking over of a country's resources without undertaking full responsibility for its government. Occasionally Britain bought certain local concessions or privileges in undeveloped countries.

Basically the only way undeveloped countries could be taken over by those with more advanced technical skills was through the use of military power or the naked threat of military power. Thus, when British troops took over a foreign country and kept its people under control, it was simple for British business interests to move in and establish profitable trade arrangements. This fact was expressed in the popular 19th-century British slogan, "Trade follows the flag."

The Suez Canal opened up the whole of Africa and Asia to British and all other European business interests. The route to the canal was, of course, the

Mediterranean Sea, and the key to the Mediterranean was still Gibraltar. With the Royal Navy the unchallenged mistress of the seas after the Battle of Trafalgar, and the Rock the impregnable guardian of the Straits of Gibraltar, the Mediterranean became virtually a British lake. Only the Royal Navy or those fleets to which the Royal Navy and the garrison at Gibraltar gave free passage could sail into and out of the Mediterranean.

The control of the Mediterranean became even more vital at the start of the 20th century when oil was discovered in the Persian Gulf area. With the invention and development of the internal-combustion engine, the world's growing need for oil created explosive economic pressures that were to turn Egypt and the rest of the Middle East into a battleground over which wars are still being fought today.

Although World Wars I and II were not directly caused by conflicting oil and other economic interests in the Middle East, the Mediterranean area was nevertheless vitally involved in these conflicts. And in both of these major holocausts Gibraltar played a key role.

11. THE ROCK'S ROLE IN
WORLD WAR I

The most imperialistic of all of the countries of continental Europe at the turn of the 20th century was Germany. After hundreds of years of disunity, the German Empire had finally become a unified nation under Otto von Bismarck, the Iron Chancellor. A new spirit of nationalism swept through the Second Reich, a spirit that was much like that of the First Reich under Charlemagne at the beginning of the 9th century. It was also a spirit that was later to sweep through Adolf Hitler's Third Reich and result in World War II.

Under Bismarck, Germany's industries and military might were built up at home, while neighboring states were taken over by diplomatic maneuver or by conquest. Neighboring states that the Germans took over included the Danish provinces of Schleswig and Holstein, and the French region of Alsace-Lorraine. In addition, Bismarck began to establish a colonial empire in Africa, Asia and in the Pacific. It was in the Mediterranean area that German interests and British interests began to collide.

By the 1890's, Germany had become the center of military and economic power on the European continent and was attempting to become Europe's greatest naval power. The British reacted violently to this challenge to their control of the seas. They viewed it as a naked bid by Germany for world supremacy.

The British Mediterranean stronghold at Gibraltar had become the most important link in a chain of bases that included Malta and Cyprus and extended into Egypt. Garrisons at these bases were kept on the constant alert against any attempt that might be made to seize the Suez Canal, which had become the thin lifeline of the British Empire. Despite other commitments at home and abroad, Britain stationed 200,000 seasoned troops on a combat-ready status in defense of the Suez Canal.

Late in the 19th century, William Gladstone, who was Prime Minister of England during the latter part of Queen Victoria's reign, had ordered Gibraltar's defenses to be strengthened. Gladstone was far from being a favorite of Queen Victoria, partially because he was unenthusiastic about her idea of extending the rule of Great Britain around the world. Nevertheless, he was shrewd enough to recognize that the Queen and the British people regarded the Rock as one of the keystones of the British Empire to be maintained at all costs.

The work on what was hoped would be the final consolidation of the Rock's defenses began shortly before Queen Victoria's Diamond Jubilee celebration, in 1897. In the strengthening of Gibraltar's interior fortifications, additional tunnels to those that had been blasted out of the Rock back during Sergeant Ince's day were excavated. Coaling yards and breakwater defenses against torpedo attacks were also completed. The main harbor was deepened and several drydocks were built to hold the largest of the world's battleships.

Under Gladstone the fortress of Gibraltar moved into the modern era. By the outbreak of World War I in 1914, the Rock was in as complete a state of readiness as it had been since the days of the Great Siege — or so it seemed.

There now arose, however, a serious question as to Gibraltar's continued strategic value. This question was caused by tremendous artillery improvements, many of which had grown out of the American Civil War of the 1860's. The most important of these improvements was the development of the rifled, breech-loading cannon.

Until the 1860's, cannons and rifles or muskets were muzzle-loaded, and the bores of the guns through which the ammunition was fired were smooth. Shells fired from smooth-bore guns met with a tremendous amount of resistance from the air and, as late as Nelson's day, they were inaccurate at any distance over 1,000 yards. (Sometimes cannonballs could actually be seen flying through the air, as they had been seen by young "Shot" and "Shell" during the Great Siege. Even when cannonballs could not actually be seen, the wind often caused them to curve in the air, somewhat as a baseball curves.) When the principle of rifling was introduced, the day of the free-flying, inaccurate cannonball was at an end.

Rifling consisted of cutting spiral grooves and raising ridges called *lands* inside the cannon barrels. The rifling gave the cannon shells a corkscrew spin when they were fired from the big guns. This spin enabled the shells to cut through the air and travel faster and farther and with greater accuracy than ever before.

Breech loading was simply a method developed for loading cannons at the breech rather than through the end of the muzzle. It grew out of the breech-loading, flintlock rifle that had been developed by an American, John Hall, in 1810.

Another important development in the improvement of artillery was the all-steel gun. Invented by Alfred Krupp, one of the founders of the great German munitions and weapons-of-war empire, the all-steel gun was first put on display in 1850. Soon all the nations of the world were attempting to copy it.

Before Krupp's gun came into use most cannon

barrels were made of solid cast iron, brass or bronze through which a tube was bored after the barrel was cast. When a gun was in use, the barrel became hot after only a few rounds had been fired, causing the barrel to become scored and useless. Early gun barrels had only a limited life.

Steel barrels, on the other hand, expanded and contracted quickly from the heat of shells being fired through them and the rapid cooling that followed when the firing stopped. Steel barrels could also have their cores or tubes, through which a shell was to be fired, built into them at the factory.

The all-steel Krupp gun had a much longer life than any gun that had preceded it. In addition, "liners," or removable steel-alloy gun casings, were soon developed. When these casings reached the end of their usefulness, they could be quickly and cheaply replaced by a new alloy liner. The Krupp gun was as important a step in the development of artillery — both on land and at sea — as the rapid-fire machine gun that was to change completely the nature of land warfare during World War I.

With all of these improvements in artillery, military men began to wonder if the Rock could not be rendered useless as a fortress by long-range guns fired from battleships or from the Spanish mainland. Spain, however, remained neutral during World War I despite the fact that many Spanish people were pro-German. One of the leaders of this pro-German faction, General Primo de Rivera, went so far as to make a fiery speech in 1917 about the recovery of Gibraltar, but Spanish officials removed him from his post. Long-range guns fired at the fortress of Gibraltar from enemy battleships never became a serious problem in World War I because Britain remained mistress of the seas, despite the new menace of the submarine.

Actually the introduction of the long-range gun worked in favor of the Rock's defenders. With it they could, for the first time, fire on enemy ships in the Straits of Gibraltar. Prior to that, the Gibraltar guns could barely reach enemy ships on the far side of the bay. Now, however, the Rock had become a truly formidable fortress with its powerful long-range guns threatening all visible land and sea surfaces.

The one weapon of war that the Gibraltar guns could not defeat was the submarine, which along with the airplane had suddenly made warfare three-dimensional. Until the introduction of these two modern weapons, wars had been two-dimensional — that is fought along the surface of the earth or sea. Now the airplane could fly and fight in the sky overhead and the submarine could sail and fight under the surface of the sea.

Near Britain's shores German submarines sank so much Allied shipping during the war that Britain was almost driven to her knees. At one point, shortly after America entered the war, there was only a three-week supply of food in the British Isles. It was at this point that Admiral William S. Sims of the United States and Britain's First Sea Lord, Admiral John Jellicoe,

worked out a system for escorting convoys of merchant
ships with cruisers and destroyers.

Before the development of the convoy system
merchant ships sailing alone had only two methods of
defending themselves against being torpedoed by submarines. One was through the use of camouflage, that
is painting the ship's hull with zebralike stripes and
other designs in the hope that the crew of an attacking
submarine would not be able to distinguish the exact
outline of the merchant ship and thus the torpedoes
would miss their mark. The second method was for
the merchant ship to sail a zigzag course and thus
avoid any torpedoes that might have found their mark
if the ship had been traveling in a straight line.

Neither of these methods of *passive* defense was
very effective. Experienced submariners were seldom
confused by even the most elaborate methods of
camouflage. Sailing a zigzag course had several draw-
backs. It was time-consuming. Occasionally, when a
merchant vessel altered its direction, it inadvertently
moved directly into a submarine's path. In addition,
if a ship were sailing a preset zigzag course — as most
ships did — the enemy submarine would simply follow
the merchant ship long enough to determine what the
pattern of this preset course was and then the death-
dealing torpedoes would be fired unerringly at their
target.

If a submarine surfaced, it was somewhat vulnerable to a merchantman's guns, but few submarines
surfaced within range of these guns or, for that matter,

surfaced at all during an engagement. The submarine simply rose to periscope depth so that the target could be sighted, and then the torpedoes were fired while the U-boat remained under water.

What was needed was some sort of *active* defense against the submarine menace, some method of forcing the enemy U-boats to attack Allied warships so the warships could deal with them by shelling them with long-range guns, or by dropping depth charges directly over the submarines as they lay beneath the surface of the sea or, as a last resort, by ramming them if they were near the surface. The answer proved to be the convoy system, which challenged the U-boats to attack the warships protecting the merchant ships.

Before Admiral Sims insisted that the convoy system be put into operation the British had opposed it. They did not like using modern warships and merchant ships together in a convoy because of the differences in the speeds of the two types of vessels. There was a great risk of ships colliding in mixed convoys, especially at night, and when warships had to slow down or circle a slow-moving convoy during the day they became instant prey for the lurking enemy submarines.

The Royal Navy's main objection, however, was based on the fact that it simply did not have the necessary escort cruisers and destroyers to spare for convoy duty. Every available British warship was engaged in combat duty against the German war fleet of surface ships. This problem was solved when

Admiral Sims assured Admiral Jellicoe that the United States would supply the necessary warships to escort the merchant ships.

A first trial convoy of merchant ships assembled at Gibraltar early in May, 1917. Escorted by American destroyers and submarine chasers, the convoy arrived safely in the British Isles on May 20. Soon afterward, the convoy system was successfully adopted by the Allies for most merchant ships as well as for troop ships, and losses decreased dramatically in British home waters.

It was the convoy system, however, that defeated the submarine, not the guns of Gibraltar — and this defeat took place mainly in the Atlantic and in British home waters, not in the Mediterranean. The first German submarines sailed serenely under the Straits in 1915. From that point until the end of the war they caused havoc among British merchant shipping. In fact, the submarine was never defeated in this area as it was elsewhere. Almost half of all Allied wartime shipping losses occurred in the Mediterranean.

This lack of success in the antisubmarine campaign in the Mediterranean was mainly due to the fact that this area was under several separate commands, and there was constant difficulty in coordinating orders on how merchant ships should be protected from the German U-boats. The Japanese navy, for example, had warships in the Mediterranean and these were offered to the Allies for escort duty. There was bickering and delay over whether this offer should be accepted and then, if accepted, who was to be in overall command of the convoy operations – the Japanese or the British. Before the argument could be settled huge losses occurred. Eventually, the Japanese did successfully protect several Allied convoys bound for such ports as Marseilles, Genoa and Port Said, but continued confusion in making command decisions prevented the Mediterranean antisubmarine campaign from being as successful as that waged in the Atlantic and British home waters where Admiral Sims and Admiral Jellicoe and their staffs worked together as a close-knit team. (Originally some thought was given to spreading submarine nets across the Straits, but the current there was too swift.)

In the last month of the war more than a dozen German U-boats sailed from the Mediterranean bound for Germany. Despite the fact that the Gibraltar gunners as well as Allied airplanes, cruisers, destroyers and other warships were alerted, all of the enemy undersea boats sailed safely through the Straits and arrived at their home ports. This was final proof, if any were needed, that submarines of this era were virtually invulnerable so long as they traveled far below the surface of the sea and were not forced into attacking surface warships. Later, of course, during World War II, highly sophisticated devices for detecting submarines were developed, but even then the convoy system proved to be the most successful method for protecting tankers, troop and merchant ships.

Despite the fact that the guns of Gibraltar were of little or no use against submarines traveling through the Straits in World War I, the Rock was the central assembly point for convoys and their escorts, and thus it was the heart of the antisubmarine campaign. In fact, if Great Britain had not held Gibraltar so that it could be used as headquarters for the convoy system, it is quite possible that the Allies would have lost the war. By the end of the war, the Rock had become such an extremely important United States naval base that many American sailors regarded the venerable fortress as their "home" port.

12. THE ROCK'S ROLE IN WORLD WAR II

Shortly after World War I ended, Spain again began to become interested in regaining possession of the Rock. This renewed interest was based on a suggestion made by Spanish engineers that a tunnel might be built under the Straits of Gibraltar that would connect the European mainland with Africa.

It was soon discovered that such a tunnel was impractical. The Straits at their narrowest point, which is called The Gut, are only eight-and-a-half miles wide, but the waters in The Gut are 2,000 feet deep. A tunnel with an incline gradual enough so that it

could be used by a railway or by vehicular traffic
would have to be 25 miles long. An exploratory shaft
for such an under-the-Straits tunnel was actually
sunk, but the project was finally abandoned.

The Spanish, however, did not give up their
renewed interest in regaining the Rock. In 1923 Primo
de Rivera became dictator of Spain, and he immediately began to make proposals to Britain for the ex-
change of Gibraltar for Ceuta. These proposals were
debated in Parliament and then politely declined.

During the Spanish Civil War fought between
1936 and 1939, and in which a number of American
volunteers took part, the Spanish dictator, General
Francisco Franco, made threatening military gestures
against the Rock. He ordered guns mounted that
would command the Bay and Straits of Gibraltar, and
in other ways indicated that he was about to retake
the great Mediterranean bastion.

No actual attempt was made against the Rock,
but the threat caused the British government once
again to improve the Gibraltar defenses. Docks were
enlarged — this time to take not only the largest battleships in the Royal Navy, but also aircraft carriers such
as the *Ark Royal*, which was to harbor at Gibraltar
during World War II. Several batteries of antiaircraft
guns were installed on the top of the Rock, concrete
gun emplacements, called pillboxes, were also installed
and, in 1938, work was begun on the all-important airplane landing strip — the strip on which General
Eisenhower's plane, the *Red Gremlin*, was to land just

a few years later. This airstrip was built across part of the old neutral ground on the isthmus that separated Gibraltar from the Spanish mainland.

When World War II actually began, Hitler urged General Franco to join the war on the side of the Axis Powers, but Franco refused. Franco's refusal was not based on any loyalty to Britain and the other Allies. It was based on the fact that Franco could not get Hitler to agree to replace the supplies of goods that Spain would lose if she were blockaded by the British Royal Navy. Spain remained a neutral throughout World War II, although her sympathies were all with Germany.*

Almost the entire civilian population of Gibraltar — some 17,000 people — was evacuated from Gibraltar shortly after World War II began. These evacuees, mostly women and children, were sent to Britain. An interesting point about their evacuation was the fact that most of the Gibraltarians, who all of their lives had been referring to Britain as "home," had never before been in the British Isles!

---

* An interesting sidelight on the neutrality of Spain during World War II was the fact that she served as a haven for Allied airmen who were shot down over Germany or German-occupied France and who managed to escape capture and make their way into Spain. When these "escapees," as they were called, were taken into custody in Spain, they were immediately imprisoned. There was an understanding, however, between Spain and the American and British governments, that these escapees could be released from jail for a fee of $10,000 — in gold. When this was paid, the escapees were promptly released and returned to Britain.

Despite the fact that there was a desperate war on and accommodations were extremely difficult to obtain, the people from Gibraltar were well taken care of in some of the best hotels in London, in private homes and in 40 evacuation centers that had been made ready for them by the Ministry of Health.

With the civilian population evacuated, Gibraltar was stripped for combat action. By 1940 the Rock was an isolated Allied island surrounded by the enemy. The entire north coast of the Mediterranean was controlled by the Axis powers. Italian troops were in North Africa and preparing to attack Egypt. Spies reported that Germany was planning to attack Gibraltar by way of Spain.

British military men knew that the garrison on the Rock would be especially vulnerable to air attack. There was only one answer to such a threat, and that was to greatly extend the tunnels inside the Rock so the whole garrison could live and work there if necessary. This work was begun in 1940 and by the time it was completed in 1942 the interior of the great limestone fortress was honeycombed with galleries containing an underground city — hospitals, elevators, electric kitchens, laundries, gasoline storage tanks, ammunition dumps, radio sending and receiving stations, workshops, and quarters for thousands of men.

The tunnels were large enough so that trucks hauling supplies could be driven through them. Great stores of supplies — food, water, medicines — were stockpiled in the event of siege. In all, about 30 miles of tunnels — more than the total mileage of surface roads on the Rock — were blasted through Gibraltar during World War II.

Although miners and tunnelers from all parts of the British Commonwealth were imported into Gibraltar for this work, those mainly responsible for it were tunneling units of the Royal Canadian Engineers, many of whose members were Canadian hardrock miners.

Canadian miners had done much tunneling work in World War I on the Western Front when mines were laid under enemy trenches, packed with high explosives and then blown up. At the start of World War II some thought had been given to using Canadian mining methods that consisted of diamond-drilling long horizontal holes into which high explosive charges could be packed. The idea was to destroy the concrete-and-steel gun emplacements in Germany's famed Siegfried Line. Germany's early military victories on the continent, however, quickly put an end to any opportunity of this kind.

In the fall of 1940, 100 members of the Royal Canadian Engineers' No. 1 Tunneling Company were sent to Gibraltar in response to a request from the Rock's garrison for experienced hardrock miners to work on extending the galleries. These were the first Canadian troops who had ever served on the Rock of Gibraltar. These and other Canadians who soon joined them were the first to use diamond-drilling methods on the great limestone Rock.

The Canadian soldier-miners' main achievement
was the carving out of a huge subterranean hospital,
which was named after Field Marshal Viscount Gort,
who was then Governor of Gibraltar. To accomplish
this feat the miners had to blast their way from the

The Gibraltar Key which was presented to the Canadian tunnellers who served on the Rock during World War II —CANADIAN GEOGRAPHICAL JOURNAL

east face to the west face of the Rock, a task that took almost two years. When it was finished the hospital was unique in military history. Sheltered from bombs by the hundreds of feet of rock overhead, it had several wards each of which were two hundred feet long, thirty-five feet wide, and twelve feet high. One twelve-hundred-foot-long tunnel leading to the hospital was named Harley Street, after the street in London where leading physicians have their offices.

Over 1½ million tons of rock from these excavations were used to extend the 1,000-foot airstrip some 800 additional yards into the sea. Additional rock (called "scree") was taken from the face of Gibraltar for work on the new runways. When the final extension on the airstrip was completed, the runways were long enough to accommodate not only Allied fighter planes but also the largest Allied bombers. All during the war, the airfield served as an invaluable staging base for planes bound for the Middle East and Malta. During the early stages of the Allied landings in North Africa in November, 1942, air support was supplied exclusively from the Rock's airstrip. During much of the war, as General Eisenhower saw when he landed there to direct Operation Torch, every inch of available space on the airfield was covered with planes of all types, sizes and description.

Although there were several anxious moments for the garrison at Gibraltar during World War II, when it seemed that invasion was inevitable, no invasion attempt was ever made. Hitler called off his plan to

UPPER LEFT:
Drilling in the interior of the Rock—CANADIAN GEOGRAPHICAL
JOURNAL

LOWER LEFT:
Dumping rock into the Mediterranean to extend the airstrip—
CANADIAN GEOGRAPHICAL JOURNAL

ABOVE:
A Canadian hard-rock miner at work on "Gib"—CANADIAN
GEOGRAPHICAL JOURNAL

Canadians at work outside Monkey's Cave where legend says the Barbary apes arrived at Gibraltar from Africa—CANADIAN GEOGRAPHICAL JOURNAL

Inside a workshop built by Canadians in the interior of Gibraltar—CANADIAN GEOGRAPHICAL JOURNAL

Interior construction work on one ward of the Gort hospital
—CANADIAN GEOGRAPHICAL JOURNAL

try to take the Rock because Franco would not grant permission for the German army to march across Spanish soil. Occasional air raids were launched against the Rock but these, for the most part, were minor affairs. The largest air attack was launched on September 24-25, 1940, when 200 Morocco-based bombers attacked the Rock. Little damage and few casualties resulted.

Gibraltar's civilian evacuees suffered few casualties in London during the two periods of intense aerial bombardment — the "great blitz" of August, 1940, when the *Luftwaffe* tried to destroy London prior to an invasion attempt, and the "little blitz" in the spring of 1944 when London was assaulted with pilotless flying bombs and rocket bombs. Londoners often said, "If you want to be safe, go and live with the Gibraltar evacuees. They're very lucky."

Nevertheless, when the flying-bomb attacks were at their peak, the Gibraltar evacuees were moved again, this time to camps in Northern Ireland. They remained there until late in the war, when they gradually began to return to the Rock. The home-coming was a joyous one, for no matter how often the intensely loyal people of Gibraltar might speak of the British Isles as home, home was truly "Old Gib" — as it had been since Rooke took the Rock in 1704.

13. THE ROCK TODAY

Anyone born on the Rock of Gibraltar has the right to be a British subject. This has been true since 1830, when the Rock first became a Crown Colony. Today the population numbers about 25,000 Gibraltarians, who are the descendants of British soldiers and sailors as well as being a fusion of many Mediterranean nationalities — Spanish, Genoese Italians, Maltese, Moroccan and Portuguese. The exact number of troops in the Gibraltar garrison is secret military information, but it probably varies between 7,000 and 10,000.

The civilian Gibraltarians are bilingual, speaking

The Convent. As has been the case for centuries, Changing of the Guard takes place here every Monday morning. C. MONTEGRIFFO

English and Spanish with equal fluency. Although they regard themselves as neither Spanish nor British, the Gibraltarians are fiercely loyal to the British Crown and the British way of life. This was dramatized in the fall of 1967 when a local referendum was held to determine if the residents of the Rock wanted to continue to be British subjects.

This referendum grew out of what was in effect

the 15th siege in the history of the Rock. In April, 1964, a Constitutional Conference was held at Gibraltar. The purpose of this conference was to give the Gibraltarians a greater voice in their own government. Serious thought was also given by Great Britain to letting Gibraltar become completely independent.

Slate water catchment, on east face of the Rock, for collecting rainwater—C. MONTEGRIFFO

During the course of the conference, however, it became clear that while the people of Gibraltar were keenly interested in self-determination, they did not really want to become wholly independent of Britain. As a result, Gibraltar continued to be a Crown Colony, but the local citizens were given much more opportunity to govern themselves under the Constitution that had been originally granted the Rock in 1950.

Shortly after the Constitutional Conference was held in 1964, the Spanish government began to reassert what it regarded as its historic claim to Gibraltar. In doing so the Spaniards insisted that the Treaty of Utrecht had been broken by the British.

"Having studied the reforms that the British Government proposes to introduce in Gibraltar," the Spanish said, "the Government of Spain points out to the Government of Great Britain that it cannot agree with the projected reforms, since it considers that they contribute to increasing the division between what was agreed on in Utrecht and the present reality in Gibraltar."

The British reply was a blunt rejection of the Spanish claims. The reply also denied that the Treaty of Utrecht had given Spain any rights whatsoever to Gibraltar. At this point the problem of the status of the Rock was turned over to the United Nations, and there it remains, unsolved. The UN has asked that Great Britain turn Gibraltar over to Spain, but Britain has termed this request, "wholly unacceptable."

Meanwhile, the Spanish dictator, Francisco Franco, began a peaceful but nevertheless real siege of the Rock. He refused to allow most of the Spanish workers to cross the border between Spain and Gibraltar, thus eliminating the daily income of between 10,000 and 14,000 of his nationals who had customarily crossed over from Spain to Gibraltar each morning and returned to their homes in Spain each night.

This, of course, seriously handicapped the Gibraltarians, but it did not by any means cripple them. Many of the Spanish day workers in Gibraltar had done domestic and menial chores. These jobs the Gibraltarians now did themselves. The Spanish in this particular instance were doing nothing but hurting themselves.

Nevertheless, Franco continued to tighten the blockade of the Rock, and by doing so he was successful in severely cutting trade between the European mainland and Gibraltar. His restrictions also seriously hampered tourist travel, because the new Spanish regulations would not permit any vehicular traffic between the continent and the Rock. If an overland tourist wanted to travel from the European continent to the Rock, or from the Rock to the rest of Europe, he had to leave his automobile at the Spanish frontier and walk across the border.

This still left open the entries by sea or air, and these were the ways that most tourists continued to

*Ships of the
United States Navy
are shown
anchored at night
inside Gibraltar harbor*
C. MONTEGRIFFO

The SS United States
*calling at
Gibraltar for the
first time,
in February 1968*
C. MONTEGRIFFO

come to the Rock. Even so, Franco continued to complain bitterly about foreign airplanes flying over Spanish soil on their way to Gibraltar, which was virtually a necessity since there was scarcely any practical way to get to the Rock by air without flying over at least a part of Spain.

In the face of this constant harassment, the citizens of Gibraltar decided to hold a referendum to see just how loyal the Gibraltarians were to the British Crown. The results proved that the Gibraltarians were even more loyal to the British than anyone had ever imagined. The referendum was held on Sunday, September 10, 1967. The results gave Britain a 99 per cent victory, 12,138 Gibraltarians voting in favor of the Rock's remaining British while only 44 voted in favor of returning the Rock to Spain. Both Spain and the United Nations refused to accept the results of this referendum.

Despite the Spanish blockade, tourism and customs duties continued to be Gibraltar's two main sources of income in the late 1960's. While Gibraltar's year-around climate is not ideal — the discomfort of the semitropical summers is increased by a hot wind from the East called a Levanter — it is favorable enough to attract Mediterranean-bound winter vacationers not only from Britain but also from the European continent and throughout the world.

Beginning in Queen Anne's day Gibraltar was a free port — that is, there were no import duties or taxes. Today the Rock is no longer a wholly free port but only a restricted number of items are subject to

*The interior of St. Michael's Cave where the band, bugles and pipes of the Royal Ulster Rifles are shown performing a public concert—*C. MONTEGRIFFO

import duties. Even these few items, however, bring in an appreciable revenue to Gibraltar, while the fact that certain other major items are duty-free or carry only a small duty make a holiday on the Rock attractive to the bargain-minded tourists.

A panoramic view of Gibraltar
and Gibraltar harbor—C. MONTEGRIFFO

A visitor to the Rock is immediately impressed with the historic military atmosphere that enshrouds the great limestone fortress. But it is doubtful in this day of the atomic bomb that Gibraltar any longer has any major significance as a fortress. Some scientists say that the limestone Rock would simply melt away if a nuclear device were dropped over it. But local citizens and guides insist that the Rock is still impregnable — and impregnably British. If one has doubts about the truth of the latter claim, the citizens or guides point to the Rock apes that still roam the middle and upper reaches of the Rock.

It is true that there continues to be a mystery

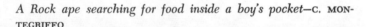

A Rock ape searching for food inside a boy's pocket—C. MON-TEGRIFFO

about these strange, simian creatures. Where they came from nobody truly knows. Some people insist that they crossed over from Africa by way of underground passageways, with their outlet being the various caves that have been discovered over the years by engineers who were drilling galleries through the Rock. Where the apes go to when they die is not known either, since skeletons of the Rock apes are almost never found. Perhaps they have their own graveyard somewhere in the legendary tunnels between Gibraltar and Africa.

In any event, while the Rock apes remain, the Rock remains British — and despite the fact that the sun has now begun to set on the British Empire — the Barbary apes have given no indication that they plan to leave the Rock. Consequently, no one really knows just how long "Old Gib" may continue to be Great Britain's only colony on the European continent and the last outpost of the British Empire.

Nevertheless, there are certain practical matters regarding the future of the Rock that must be taken into consideration by the British government. It costs Great Britain about 15 million pounds (between 35 and 40 million dollars) a year to maintain Gibraltar as a major naval base, and the Royal Navy no longer needs a base of this size. Further, the United States has a naval base at nearby Rota in Spain that meets the modern needs of the American Navy.

If the British would return Gibraltar to Spain,

Car decorated with outcome of the 1967 referendum

General Franco has said he would allow the Gibraltarians to remain on the Rock and to retain their British citizenship. He has also offered them freedom of speech and of the press as well as other basic freedoms. But the residents of the Rock refuse to trust either Franco or Spain. The ringing slogan of the fiercely loyal Gibraltarians continues to be: "British to the Core! British since 1704!"

BOOKS FOR FURTHER READING

The book I would most highly recommend to young people who wish to do further reading about Gibraltar is Dorothy Ellicott's, "From Rooke to Nelson." This, along with Mrs. Ellicott's most recent work on the history of Gibraltar during the Peninsular War, "Bastion Against Aggression," can be obtained directly from her at 1 Town Range, Gibraltar.

The classic work on the Great Siege and the one to which most modern authors are indebted is Colonel John Drinkwater's "A History of the Siege of Gibraltar, 1779-1783," published by New Edition in London in 1905. Colonel Drinkwater was a member of the garrison at Gibraltar during the Great Siege.

A more recent work on the same subject is T. H. McGuffie's, "The Siege of Gibraltar," published by Dufour Editions, Philadelphia, in 1965.

Each year an annual report on Gibraltar is issued. This paperback report gives up-to-date statistical information on the economy and government of the Rock. The most recent annual report on Gibraltar can be obtained from Her Majesty's Stationery Office, London.

Several Spanish and British white papers have been prepared that present opposing views on the international status of the Rock. These reports can be obtained from the United Nations in New York.

One of the best of the short histories of the Rock was Major A. J. L. Gache's *Gibraltar,* which appeared in the British Survey. The booklet was later reprinted in the Gibraltar Chronicle and can be obtained by writing that newspaper.

Another excellent short history is C. E. Carrington's "Gibraltar," published by the Oxford University Press, London, in 1956 and updated in 1966.

Other more advanced books of a general nature on the history of Gibraltar include the following:

ANDREWS, A. "Proud Fortress." London, Evans Brothers, Ltd., 1958.

GARRATT, G. T. "Gibraltar and the Mediterranean." London, Cape, 1939.

HOWES, DR. H. W. "The Story of Gibraltar." London, Philip Tacey, 1946.

KENYON, E. R. "Gibraltar Under Moor, Spaniard and Briton." London, Methuen, 1938.

STEWART, J. D. "Gibraltar the Keystone." Boston, Houghton Mifflin, 1967.

INDEX

poleon I), 108
"Desert Fox" (Erwin Rommel), 24
"Iron Chancellor" (Otto von Bismarck), 116
"Iron Duke" (Duke of Wellington), 108
"Little Corporal" (Napoleon I), 95
"Old Gib" (Rock of Gibraltar), 138, 151
"Sailor King" (King William IV), 64
"Shell" (Tom Richmond), 75
"Shot" (John Brand), 75
North Africa, invasion of, 11-24, 133

Old Mole, 41
Operation Sea Lion, 96
Operation Steady, 70-5
Operation Torch, 11, 12, 16, 18, 20, 23, 133
Oran, Algeria, 17, 21
Panama Canal, 112
Panther, 65
Patton, George S., 17, 21
Pearl Harbor, 20-1
penal colony, Gibraltar used as, 32-4
peninsula, site of Gibraltar, 26
Peninsular War, 107-8
Persian Gulf
  oil discovered, 115
Pétain, Henri, 20
Philip V, King, 36, 49
Pillars of Hercules, 25-6
pirates
  from Algiers, 34
  from Tarfia, 32

population of Gibraltar, 139
Port Said, Egypt, 111, 112

Queen Anne's War, 36
quotations. *See* slogans, quotations, and famous phrases

Red Gremlin, 12, 13, 128
red-hot shot, 77-89
Rédoubtable, 104
Red Sands, 72
referendum, 140-1, 146
Richmond, Tom, 75
rifling, artillery, 118-19
Rivera, Primo de, 120-1, 128
roads on Gibraltar, 131
Rock apes, 19-20, 150-1
Rodney, George, 63, 64
Rommel, Erwin, 16, 24
Rooke, George, 34-45
Roosevelt, Franklin D., 16
Rosia Harbor, 105
Ross, Charles, 70-5
Royal Canadian Engineers, 131
Royal Catherine, 39
Royal Navy, 115, 123-4, 128
  motto, 103
Royal Sovereign, 104

Said Mohammed Pasha, 111
Salinas, Diego de, 40
scurvy, 64, 90
Seven Years' War, 54, 55
Shovell, Cloudesley, 38
Shrapnel, Henry, 66
sieges
  7th, 31-2
  11th, 34, 40-4
  12th, 46-8
  13th, 49